MOTHER MEERA

ANSWERS

CONTENTS

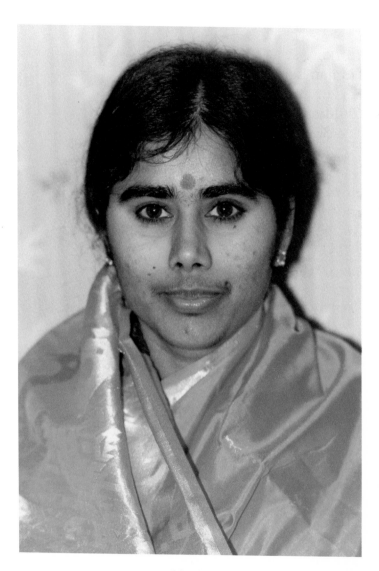

No. 22
Thalheim, Germany 1994

INTRODUCTION

The Divine Mother has always been worshipped as
the sustaining soul and force of the universe.
Although some of the faces that she wears are well
known – Kali, the Virgin Mary, Isis, for example –
many of her embodied forms have chosen to work
quietly in the world. In turbulent times such as
these, several incarnations of the Divine Mother
move among us, each with her particular task of
healing, or protection, or transformation.

One of the most widely revered and loved of
these Avatars of the Divine Mother is Mother
Meera, a young Indian woman who was born on
December 26, 1960, in the village of Chandepalle in
southern India. She soon showed herself to be an
unusual child: by the age of three she would report
«going to various lights.» Her parents treated her
as an exceptional child and loved her very much.
Her family was not especially religious and she
was not brought up in any tradition. Her real
parents were the spiritual guides that she met in
vision; it was from them that she received the love
and help she needed. The state of samadhi was
constant for her. Under the auspices of her uncle,
Mr. Reddy, she lived for some time in Pondicherry
where her extraordinary presence attracted

considerable attention. She married a German in 1982; and he stays with the Mother. She presently lives in Thalheim, a quiet village in Germany. Although she has not sought publicity, thousands of people from all over the world come to receive her darshan, her silent bestowal of grace and light through her gaze and touch. Mother Meera is worshipped as a Divine Mother in India.

The unique gift of Mother Meera to the world is to make available for the first time in the history of the Earth the radically transformative Light of Paramatman, the Supreme Being. In this time of crisis and growing spiritual hunger, the Mother offers her children a direct transmission of Light that dissolves all barriers and changes the entire being. This Light can be received by all who are open, whether or not they have met the Mother in the body.

As an incarnation of the Divine Mother, Mother Meera stands above all dogmas and hierarchies. She asks no special allegiance, and offers her transformative power to all, no matter what their path or religion.

Answers is at once Mother Meera's own answers to the questions devotees have put to her over many years concerning her identity, her work, and her way, and an account of the working of the

Divine Mother in the world. The questions and answers were collected by Christine Cox, Jeffrey Cox, Adilakshmi, Mother Meera's secretary and devotee, as well as other devotees. Adilakshmi interjected some wonderful comments that have been retained in this book.

The Divine Mother is in a body, offering in this hardest of times a path of joy and transformation, a chance to open to her blessing, to receive and work with her light, to change ourselves and the world in which we live.

«The whole purpose of my work is in the calling down of the Paramatman Light and in helping people. For this I came – to open your hearts to the Light.»

THE WORK OF MOTHER MEERA

Question: The work of the Mother in the world is going on all the time now, isn't it?

Mother Meera: All the time. The consciousness of mankind is being prepared for great leaps and discoveries – in a gentle way wherever possible. But some things will have to be destroyed. I do not like to destroy; I like to change things. But where there is no openness there must be destruction. However, God is giving man a great chance. Many divine persons are here. We are showing man a way out; we are offering him the divine Light, the divine knowledge. We are bringing down into the consciousness of the Earth the divine consciousness. Now man must choose. Man is free; God will not force his children to do anything. He wants their free love. Mercy and love are always there.

Q: You have brought down the Paramatman Light to help speed the work of world and individual transformation. Is there an aspect to your work other than that of bringing down the Light?

MM: I have come to say that all paths are as good as each other and all lead to the Divine, and that therefore the various believers should respect each other's ways. For example, Muslims, Christians, Hindus, Buddhists, and other religious people can believe and follow their own faith, but should not hate or fight others' faith. People who follow any path can come to me – I help them to remember the Divine, and give them peace and happiness when they are in trouble.

Q: What is your main purpose?

MM: It is to help humans and to make them happy, peaceful, contented, harmonious, and loving. Happiness and spiritual growth are connected. Being peaceful and being happy form the most important foundation of spiritual practice. Then the practice goes by itself.

Q: What is your aim?

MM: To protect all aspects of the human being.

Adilakshmi: Mother Meera understands human nature totally and knows how difficult it is on Earth. She helps all types of people whatever their life situation or stage of awareness. Other incarnations tend to focus their help on those on one stage of life.

Q: I am afraid, Mother, that when people come to see you they interfere with your work. Is that true?

MM: Nothing can and nothing will interfere with my work. If the whole world came to me, my work would not be interrupted or deflected for a moment. I am working on all planes. I am working everywhere. This Earth is only one of the planes where I am working. How could anything disturb my work?

Q: Will your work unfold over the centuries and will it be long remembered?

MM: Yes.

Q: Will things in the world change, because of your presence here, in an inner or an outer way?

MM: In both ways.

Q: Do you feel a need to enlighten the world quickly?

MM: I am not in a hurry. When the world wants to come, it will.

Q: Do you want to begin a religion?

MM: No. The Divine is the sea. All religions are rivers leading to the sea. Some rivers wind a great deal. Why not go to the sea directly?

BRINGING DOWN THE PARAMATMAN LIGHT

Q: What is the importance of the Paramatman Light?

MM: I called down the Paramatman Light. The Paramatman Light is in everything. The work of transformation will be done much more quickly, providing people are open. Even if they are not open now, the pressure and power of the Light are so great that they will become open.

Q: What does it mean to bring down the Paramatman Light? Isn't Paramatman already everywhere?

MM: The Paramatman Light is everywhere, but when one needs it one must know when, where, how, and for what to use it. The Light was always there; I prayed to Paramatman, the Supreme Being, to be able to use it. The Light has never been USED before. Like electricity, it is everywhere, but one must know how to activate it. I have come for that.

Q: According to The Mother *you worked with other divine beings to bring down the Paramatman Light. Was this the first time in the history of the Earth that this Light has been brought down?*

No. 26
Niagara Falls, USA 1989

MM: Mr. Reddy asked a famous pundit, a Vedic scholar, who looked through the ancient texts and said that this is indeed the first time it has been brought down.

Q: Is it your divine mind that is directing the Paramatman Light?

MM: It is not helpful to use words like *mind*; the process simply takes place.

Q: Do you bring down lights from different planes or do you work with the Paramatman Light alone?

MM: I work with the Light of Paramatman as well as with lights from the planes of Gods and Goddesses.

Q: Did you have to be in the world for this Light to enter it?

MM: Yes.

Q: If you leave your body, will the Light leave with you?

MM: It will stay, it will continue. Each Avatar brings down a particular Light which changes human history.

We have to try to reveal that Light which is hidden in us as a bud. It must blossom like a flower. In all things everywhere, in all beings, the

Light is hidden, and it must be revealed. If we try with all our hearts we will be successful. I want the Paramatman Light to blossom everywhere.

PARAMATMAN AND HIS LIGHT

Q: What is God?

MM: What is not God? Everything – good and bad – is God.

Q: Would you describe Paramatman?

MM: Paramatman is infinite Light, and is the source of all, of being, knowledge, bliss, of peace, of each atman, each soul.

Q: Is there a difference between Paramatman and his Light?

MM: In a way. Paramatman is in everything, in all creation – earth, water, fire, air, sky, animals – at all times. But we can see the Light only sometimes. The Light has the quality of love, grace, power, bliss, jnana. Without it, nothing can exist.

Q: *What is the Paramatman Light like?*

MM: It is colorless but has every color in it and the color and the force of every light of every plane. It is everywhere and in everything.

Q: *How do you experience Paramatman? Do you experience Him with form?*

MM: I experience Paramatman as Light. It usually is white but sometimes has color.

Q: *Are all lights from the same source?*

MM: Yes, but each guru and god has its own light with different qualities. What you receive depends on what you worship.

Q: *Can other gurus use the Paramatman Light to help their devotees?*

MM: Human gurus cannot use it. However, since Avatars come from Paramatman, they all will naturally work with the Paramatman Light. But working with the Light is not the same as bringing down the Light. I am bringing down the Light for the general protection of the life of all things and all creatures.

THE DIVINE MOTHER

Q: What is the difference between God, Shakti and the Divine Mother?

MM: Paramatman is everything; the Shakti is only a part, only a small portion of his power and Light. Paramatman creates everything, and the Shakti, Gods and Goddesses protect the creation. The Shakti is more powerful than the Divine Mother. The Shakti has no form, although we may imagine her having one. She is worshipped separately from Paramatman and is independent of our prayers – what she wants to do she will do. The Shakti cannot be controlled; when we worship her we can only surrender. On the other hand, the Divine Mother answers our prayers. She has love for humans and protects them and promotes harmony and peace.

Q: Is the Divine Mother completely surrendered to Paramatman?

MM: There is a mutual understanding between the Divine Mother and Paramatman; it is not a question of surrender.

Q: What is the difference between the Divine Mother and the Divine Father?

MM: The Father is stricter, the Mother is more loving and soft. She is more patient than the Father and more accepting.

Q: If the Buddha represents the force of illumined mind, what do you represent?

MM: I will help in every way that I am needed. The force of the Mother is that She has not one great force, but all forces.

Q: Are there other incarnations of the Divine Mother on Earth at this time?

MM: Yes, many. Some will be known, others wish to remain secret. The work of each is different. Each expresses a different aspect of the Divine Mother. My scope is very broad and more integral. I help people at all stages of life, and I also work with Sri Aurobindo and Sweet Mother.

Q: If the Divine Mother is love, why is there so much suffering in creation?

MM: Not only the Divine Mother exists but Paramatman also exists.

Q: Is the Mother force especially important now for the Earth?

MM: The Earth always needs the Mother, her Light and protection. She is a child that needs the Mother's divine help.

Q: As I understand it, Mother Earth is the being for our planet Earth. Are we humans like parts or cells of her?

MM: No, we are not parts – we are her children.

Q: What is our relationship to Mother Earth, the soul of this planet?

MM: Earth is the root for all – it gives everything. Earth gives bodies, Paramatman gives Light, and we receive both.

Q: Although the Mother has always been present, it seems that now mankind in the West is becoming increasingly conscious of the Mother on a large scale.

MM: People have always worshipped both the Divine Mother and God. Ordinary people have always believed that the Virgin Mary, for instance, is divine even though only lately the Church has formally recognized this. The importance is to open to the Divine; whether it is the Shakti or God doesn't matter.

Q: What evokes the working of the feminine aspect of God?

MM: When humans sincerely aspire for happiness, harmony, peace and light, then it is the Divine Mother who helps.

Q: Can one characterize the spiritual path guided by the feminine energy as one of transformation rather than one of transcendence?

MM: No. Transformation is one aspect of the process. Transcendence, union with the Divine, is the primary aim of the human being. The goal of the Divine Personality or Avatar is to help the human being to be in the Divine. Transformation is not the final aim – but it enables all people to attain union with God more easily.

Q: What does transformation by the Divine Mother include?

MM: She gives help for physical, mental, vital and spiritual well-being, gives peace, and helps people to obtain their needs. When humans on Earth are afflicted with difficulties, it is the Divine Mother who relieves suffering and lifts them up.

WORLD TRANSFORMATION

Q: Do all mankind's old structures, the ideas and habits, have to be transformed?

MM: Yes. But such great changes take time. They have to be worked for, aspired for. Man has to do a great labour; God will not do everything. When people become conscious of the presence of the Light, the transformation can go faster. It is working anyway, but few people are conscious. More will be conscious soon, many more, and then the work can be done with greater efficiency. But in the meantime, enjoy the Light. It is here; let it change you. The transformation will come in its own time.

Q: I see so much madness and greed in the world it is hard to believe that the transformation of man and the world is possible.

MM: What you see is real, but the goodness in man is also real. The longing for God is real – it is man's most true reality. And God loves man absolutely. The transformation will happen but it will take time and go slowly. Its foundations have to be made firm.

Q: The transformation of the world includes changing the most banal and difficult aspects of life, doesn't it?

MM: It would not be transformation if it did not mean that. Nothing must be avoided. Those who love me will work with everything in the world – all the darkness and all the difficulties. Do people imagine I do not work, or that the realized man does not work? Divine work is the hardest work, and it is without end. I am asking people to take on the whole difficulty of matter and of reality. I have come in a body to show that this is possible. My grace and help and Light are there but man must also do the work. People should not come to me if they just want to escape something. I have not come only to be a refuge; I have also come to give the joy and strength necessary for change. There are no quick answers and easy solutions.

Q: Is this world especially dear to God?

MM: All worlds are dear to God. He has the responsibility to attend to each, like a gardener to each of the gardens in a large estate.

Q: Mr. Reddy, your uncle, said that your coming to the earth meant that man was now in a position to collaborate with God in re-making the world, that he was at last evolved enough. Is this true?

MM: Yes, but he must be evolved enough to be humble. He must understand that he can do nothing without the Light. He must turn to the higher force, the force that is love and knowledge.

ABOUT MOTHER MEERA

Q: Did you incarnate knowing that you were divine?

MM: Before coming here I knew who I was, knew that I would incarnate and what my work would be. The Mother is beyond time.

Q: Have you ever been a human being?

MM: No.

Q: Did you know who you were, even as a baby?

MM: Yes, I always knew.

Q: Why do you live so normal and simple a life in a quiet German village?

MM: To show the world that the transformation is normal, can be done anywhere and in daily life.

Q: To which of the aspects of the Divine Mother mentioned by Aurobindo in his book The Mother – *Maheshwari, Mahasarasvati, Mahalakshmi, Mahakali – do you feel closest, and are there others besides these that play a part in your work?*

26

B&W No. 1
Pondicherry, India 1974

MM: I have all four aspects, but more of the quality of Durga. Durga has more patience than the others. Durga is the aspect of the Mother that loves her children more and that punishes less. She forgives. Durga loves humans more than do the other Goddesses. When Durga destroys, she destroys what is necessary, not with anger but with love. Durga will always come down to whatever level she is needed. You can think of her in many ways – as a mother, a teacher, a father.

Adilakshmi: Ma has true compassion, and true compassion is without sentiment. She knows that if she consoles our illusions she keeps us in the fire of ignorance. We who do not know love cheapen it by trying to draw it down to our level. It is harder and gentler at the same time than what we know.

Q: Do you change?

MM: My body changes and your perception of me changes as you grow in knowledge. I have always been the same and will always be the same.

Q: Do you have any desires?

MM: My deepest desire is to be with Paramatman.

Adilakshmi: When Mother is in a body, she wishes also to be totally with Paramatman. There is a great difference for her between when she is in a body and when she is with Paramatman.

Q: Mother, what is that difference?

MM: When I am in a body I must fulfill my duties towards you and the world. When I am with Paramatman, I am free from all these responsibilities.

Q: Is this your sacrifice – to give up this total union in order to be here with us?

MM: Yes.

Q: Would you say something about your experience of the world and of God?

MM: Although I may be sitting here, I have my own way of traveling to other places. Although my body is in a particular place, I can simultaneously be elsewhere – Thalheim, for example. I know past, present, and future simultaneously, so there is no duality. Awareness is always there, so there is only the One.

Q: You have often said that for you there is no «separation» at any time. What do you mean?

MM: For me there is no difference between here and there, high and low. Everything is God, every activity is divine, all the worlds and all the Gods are here.

Q: Is knowledge of any event or being available to you?

MM: On this plane or the higher planes?

Q: On this plane.

MM: What kind of information?

Q: What the president is doing right know, for example.

MM: It is not so easy. But if there is a serious problem, or someone needs help, that I can know. Situations in which my help can make a difference are the ones that I can know. But to find out something just for curiosity, no.

Q: Can you contact the souls of people who died several years ago?

MM: I can know whether the soul is in a good condition or not, but I cannot tell where the soul will be born next.

Q: People imagine that the Avatar should know everything on every plane, like a kind of supercomputer.

MM: As the Mother, I have my own special work which I know exactly and precisely how to accomplish. This has nothing to do with any other work I may do. In such other work I may at times not know. It is not my work to «know» everything, such as where a missing hammer is.

Q: Are you consciously aware of calls for your help, or does your power work automatically?

MM: The grace works automatically when the aspiration is sincere. It is not necessary for me always to know. If I had twenty telephones in this room and they were all ringing, it would not be helpful. But I can know what I want when I want and when I need.

Q: When you are asked a question, how does the answer come?

MM: I SEE it. Even as a child it was this way.

Q: Do you communicate with other divine beings?

MM: Yes.

Q: Is your state of consciousness different in darshan than it is in other times?

MM: No. Because in darshan devotees concentrate on and open to me more than usual, they feel that the energy from me is special. But my consciousness has always been the same.

Q: The day after your serious operation you received your devotees and disciples to your bedside. You use every moment to teach and show your love, don't you?

MM: This is the divine way. Ramana Maharshi gave darshan as he was dying. Anandamayima also. Every minute is used.

Q: In accepting embodiment, have you experienced much suffering and pain?

MM: Everyone suffers – the Divine, the human, even the evil forces – but at different levels. So many holy beings have suffered greatly. Christ was crucified; Aurobindo had bad trouble with his leg; Ramakrishna had throat cancer. For physical pain you can get medicine. For divine pain, what medicine is there?

Q: Can you offer up your own suffering and thus transform it?

MM: You have the chance to offer your pain to me, but I cannot offer my pain to anybody but Paramatman. Suffering comes from the Supreme; both Light and pain come from there. The Avatar has a dharma like everybody else, and must bear the pain of being an Avatar. This is my part in the play. I must do what the Supreme says.

Q: What is the Avatar's pain?

MM: Public life brings many questions and difficulties. It is painful sometimes being falsely blamed and it is hard sometimes to deal with the ignorance.

Q: By loving you more, can we help take your suffering?

MM: You cannot take my suffering. But through the love of those who come to me, I can bear it. If there is fidelity and love and sincerity and devotion I will live longer. It is the same for every Avatar; the Avatar is love and only bound by love.

Q: Are you hurt by ingratitude?

MM: Nearly always I take it lightly. On very rare occasions it is painful.

Q: Do you feel hurt when people do not take what you want to give?

MM: There is no desire to give. Let people receive whatever they can.

Q: Were you frightened, as a child, when the Light began to enter your body?

MM: No, I am never afraid. As a child I used to love going out alone into the dark. People said it was dangerous, that there were scorpions everywhere. But it never frightened me.

Q: Will you incarnate again on Earth?

MM: I do not know. It depends firstly on the sanction of Paramatman and secondarily on the strong wishes and prayers of devotees for me to incarnate.

Q: What do you see when you look in a mirror?

MM: What I see is not interesting to me.

Q: Sweet Mother of Pondicherry said that just because someone is in her personal entourage that does not mean that he or she has a deeper spiritual relationship to her. Is this the same with you?

MM: One cannot generalize. This varies according to many factors.

Q: Do you accept anyone who comes to you?

MM: I accept anyone who comes to me sincerely. I cannot turn him or her away, even if he or she causes problems. This is the Mother's way.

Q: Have some of your devotees incarnated with you before?

MM: No, but they have had relationships to the Divine. The power of the various masters is the same; what attracts the devotees are the personalities of the masters.

Q: Do you ever feel that your devotees want to possess you?

MM: Many people think they can own me, but I will always escape. I have always been, and will always be, free.

Q: Devotees often feel that you like them more or less than others or that you are angry or happy with them. Do you have feelings about the various devotees in this way?

MM: When people have to work with me, they are more likely to experience these feelings. It is not that I like one more than the other; with whom I work depends on what work needs to be done. My love is equal for all. Sometimes I become angry while working with someone who insists on doing something his or her own way when I know it will take too much time and is not good. But this anger, which is rare, arises only in work situations. I do

B&W No. 2
Pondicherry, India 1976

not become angry at a devotee who does something bad to another, for example. I change him or her.

Q: What is the best way to be with you, to be around you?

MM: Be simple, happy, and peaceful with not too many thoughts.

Q: Do you feel any special attachment to any country?

MM: Wherever there is aspiration, I will feel happy. My work is not for one country or one race or one people only; it is for the world.

Q: Mother, why do you speak so little these days about your own experiences?

MM: People can do nothing for my work until they themselves are realized. So all energy should go into that work of realization. What is the use of telling people things they cannot understand until they are realized? It might confuse them; it might make them vain or proud. What I want is complete simplicity and complete surrender; not words, not discussions, but action.

Q: What is the most profound experience for you?

MM: When people are happy, that is the most profound experience for me.

Q: The Mother has many faces: withdrawn, majestic, mischievous, angry, tender. What is the real face?

MM: All are real. But the most real is the face of love. Keep gazing on that, whatever happens. Turn to that in whatever difficulties you experience. Revere that through whatever pain you are passing, and you will be given every joy and every courage. Perfect love of the Mother is to see her face of love in everything that happens. If you attain that love, you will be able to do anything. There is a Telugu song: «Love can melt the stone, turn the mountain to water.» Perfect love can never be defeated because it is infinite.

AVATARS

Q: Avatars are incarnations of the Divine come to Earth to help her creatures. Is each Avatar an incarnation of an aspect of the Divine, or of the total Divine?

MM: God and the Avatar are in one way the same and another way different. The Avatar comes from God and has the power and Light of God. But we can differentiate because the Avatar has a human body while God has no form and yet all forms. Each Avatar is a manifestation of a part of the Divine, of Paramatman.

Q: What is the relation of Avatars to each other and to the Divine?

MM: Each Avatar can be considered as one facet of a diamond, and at the same time the whole diamond. What we see is one facet, but the whole diamond is behind it and around it.

Q: Is each Avatar given a specific sphere of influence and a particular task?

MM: Yes, each Avatar has a different task to fulfill.

Q: Are all Avatars equally powerful?

MM: All Avatars and gurus have the same purpose of uplifting humanity towards God, but the ways are different and the paths and techniques are different.

Q: Why do Westerners find it difficult to believe in Avatars?

MM: Westerners give excessive importance to the material world view. Because their material lives proceed systematically, they have little time or impetus to consider the possibility of an Avatar.

Even when an Avatar comes, many Westerners are not willing to give the time to meet him or her.

Q: Even thoughtful Western philosophers have denied that the Divine could incarnate in human form at all.

MM: The Avatar is nevertheless a direct incarnation of God.

Q: Can the whole Divine incarnate in a body?

MM: You cannot say that the whole of Paramatman is in the Avatar's body because the body is a limitation, whereas Paramatman is limitless. The Avatar incarnates a part of the Divine but can call upon any of the divine powers it needs at any moment for any purpose.

Q: Mr. Reddy once said that a human realized guru is just one fingernail on one of the thousand hands of the Avatar. Is this so?

MM: Yes, the Avatar's power to change things is very much greater.

Q: How can we help others to understand this?

MM: With explanation you can try to convince people, but often this will be difficult. But once they have the experience, no words are necessary.

Q: What is the relationship between an Avatar and the world?

MM: Avatars, like God, don't expect anything from devotees or the world. They go on doing their work regardless of the response of the world to them. Although God sends Avatars to earth, humans often don't understand that the being is an Avatar. Perhaps only for a fraction of a second do they see.

Q: Can you say what the general work is of Avatars for the world and for humans?

MM: Generally, when people ask Avatars for something, they will be helped. Avatars help humans who are having difficulties and suffering, and turn people from wrong paths. They come to help beings of all types: animals, plants, humans, and creatures in all the five elements.

The possibility for mankind to evolve and change is always there whether or not an Avatar comes. People naturally believe in a greater reality. However, when an Avatar comes people feel the possibility more and aspire more strongly.

Q: If we could see you in cosmic vision as Arjuna saw Krishna, would we see the entire Divine Mother in her glory around you?

MM: Each individual will have a unique way of seeing the Avatar.

Q: You have said that there are both Mothers and Fathers. What kind of force do the Fathers bring down, and how is it different from that of the Mothers?

MM: All Avatars come from the same source, and the Light they bring down is the same. However, the purposes of each incarnation are different. But both male and female may work for peace, or transformation, or harmony, for example.

Q: Do Avatars know right from the beginning that they are divine, or do they come slowly into that realization? For example, wasn't it only later in Jesus' life that he understood his divine mission?

MM: Jesus knew from the beginning that he was the son of God. The changing experiences in an Avatar's life have more to do with making it clear to the world who he or she is.

Q: What, specifically, did Jesus and Krishna bring to the Earth?

MM: Jesus symbolized sacrifice. Krishna brought love and peace, and destroyed some of the asuras of the time.

Q: Is the Virgin Mary an Avatar?

MM: There is no doubt about it.

Q: What aspects of the Divine Mother does she particularly express?

MM: She expresses compassion.

Q: There is a great upsurge of interest in the Virgin throughout the Catholic Church. Can you say something about the purpose of her work?

MM: Mary has the quality of Motherhood; she is appearing to protect her children.

Q: Is it really the Virgin who is appearing at Medjugorje, Yugoslavia?

MM: Yes, she is appearing in Medjugorje.

Q: Will the Virgin or Jesus incarnate again?

MM: Because people find it difficult to believe that an embodied form could really be Jesus and Mary, they are coming as appearances such as that at Medjugorje.

Q: How is it possible that Avatars become sick? Surely they don't have personal karma!

MM: Avatars do have a particular karma. Since they are in the world, they have bodies of the same material as do others. The bodies are subject to nature's laws, with their inevitable suffering. Sometimes Avatars take care of disciples and do not take care of themselves; sometimes Avatars take on the karma of disciples. But the pain experienced by Avatars is not felt so deeply, is not experienced as suffering.

Q: Being an Avatar is a job, isn't it?

MM: Yes, it is one kind of divine life. I do what Paramatman tells me. If he tells me to come down, I come down.

Q: Could an Avatar be said to be realized?

MM: Realization is not a word that can be used of a person who has come directly from the Divine, but only of those who have something to attain, that is, of human beings.

Q: How is the work of an Avatar different from that of a self-realized guru?

MM: Avatars come from the Divine, while self-realized persons go to the Divine. Avatars are always one with God and never lose awareness of the Divine, unlike gurus who began ignorant. To become self-realized, people – through spiritual practice, meditation, and japa – work hard and then reap the fruit. Since they have worked strenuously, they expect others to work as they have; they do not have as much patience as do divine personalities. Also, Avatars can change things faster.

TEACHERS AND GURUS

Q: Should we follow gurus?

MM: It depends on the guru. In exceptional circumstances, a guru might be necessary, even vital for spiritual development. Generally it is best to pray to the Supreme directly, or approach Him through one of His divine incarnations. That is more useful. If any human guru is giving you teachings that bring you closer in your heart to the Divine, listen and be grateful and follow them. But be clear about the limitations of all human gurus. They can only point the way; they cannot take you there. If you want to see the Divine, why don't you ask Him directly?

Q: An Avatar can give light. Cannot a guru do this also?

MM: Yes, a guru can also give light, but it is a different kind of light.

Q: Why do some Avatars, such as Sai Baba, perform «miracles»?

MM: To attract the mind and lead it towards God.

Q: How can we tell if a guru is genuine?

MM: If we feel peace and bliss in his or her presence, this is a sign that a guru can help us. But if we go to a guru and do not feel anything, this does not mean that the guru has nothing to give, but only that we do not need at this time what she or he has to offer. The relationship of guru and disciple depends on how much the guru can help a particular disciple at his or her current stage of development. At a certain stage in the development, the relation with the guru is over and then the disciple goes to another guru. A guru has all capacities for teaching and can be capable of being simultaneously a kindergarten teacher to one student and a university professor to another.

Q: In traditional times it was often very difficult to see a Master. Why is it easier now?

MM: It is still difficult. People may come to me, but to recognize that an Avatar is an Avatar needs years of real aspiration and tapasya.

Q: Everyone's way to you is different, isn't it?

No. 21
Thalheim, Germany 1994

MM: Yes. Each child loves the Mother with its own temperament, its own nature. And the Mother loves each child according to its own nature.

Adilakshmi: Some have seen the Mother as Buddha, some as Krishna, some as the Virgin Mary. Some have had visions from her in Hindu terms, some in Buddhist, some Christian. She will teach the soul in whatever ways are most familiar to it.

OPENING TO THE LIGHT

Q: When people ask for your help you simply say yes. How do you help them?

MM: There are different lights which serve different purposes. I send whichever light is needed.

Q: What are the different lights and what are the characteristics of each?

MM: Golden and white lights are the lights of Paramatman, and are the main ones. The other lights belong to Avatars, Gods and Goddesses. The light of Durga is red and is characterized by power. The blue light is Krishna and is the light of knowledge and love. Violet light is for physical health.

Green is the color of the life force in the material world. Orange is the color of sacrifice, the color of sannyasins.

Q: How can a devotee be the most receptive to your Light?

MM: When people have a silent mind they will receive more. When they are restless, they cannot feel what I am giving. I give what I can and what the person needs anyway, but if the person is silent, he or she can become aware of the process.

Q: I get the impression from reading The Mother *that there is a specific moment when one receives any of the Lights – the Supramental or Paramatman. Isn't one always receiving them to some degree?*

MM: Humans do not receive the Light continuously, but only at special moments, such as in darshan. During pranam and darshan the action of the Light is to create a balance between wordly and spiritual life. Apart from darshan, there are rare moments of reception of the Light that bring the devotee rapid spiritual growth.

Q: How do we receive the Light and what do we feel when we receive it?

MM: People receive it in many ways. Some receive it through the head, some through the fingers – what do details matter? It is the effect that matters: an unmistakable and extraordinary lightness and happiness and peace. The Supramental Light can burn slightly when you receive it; the Supreme Light does not hurt. You can receive the Light anywhere and at any time. Knowing that, open to it without delay. There is no time to waste.

Q: At what stage of the spiritual practice do we perceive the Paramatman Light directly?

MM: I cannot say at what level you will be when you see it. It depends on your strong aspiration to see it and also on the maturity of your practice. It is the aim of human beings to see the Paramatman Light, first to see it and then to merge with it.

Q: What blocks us from perceiving the Light?

MM: You have your duties and cannot concentrate only on the Paramatman Light. When the time comes, nothing will stop you from seeing it.

Q: Can you describe the experience of opening to the Light?

MM: The Light always brings happiness. The Light can enter through any part of the body and can be felt in many ways. We cannot generalize – people may feel pain at first or may not feel it in the body at all.

The results of the Light entering are many. You experience happiness, even if you were suffering before. When you work you do so without strain and attachment. Although you don't feel that you are doing anything, the results of the work will be good. You have less enthusiasm for work, but you can accomplish more because the work goes easily.

Q: Sometimes the Light comes with such intensity I feel that I will not survive.

MM: The Light always works within one's limits.

Q: Does your Light itself bring understanding?

MM: Those who come to me for darshan receive whatever they need – knowledge does not necessarily come with the Light. When our devotion, surrender, and humility grow deeper and deeper, then knowledge will come from Paramatman and will make things clearer and clearer.

Q: What is the relationship of peace and bliss to the Light?

MM: They come from the Light. Which ones you experience depends on your personality, your past karma, your state of consciousness, and which path is yours – bhakti, karma, jnana and so forth.

Q: How can I open to those aspects of the Light – peace and bliss – that I don't currently experience?

MM: Meditate. Do japa on one of the names of the Divine – this can be done anywhere.

Q: As we understand more, does our karma lessen?

MM: Yes. The more you go into the Light, the less your karma becomes, and when you realize yourself, it disappears.

ASPECTS OF THE PATH

Q: Is everything in this yoga really done by the Divine?

MM: Yes. Everything comes from the top down.

Q: Why do you teach in silence?

MM: People want lectures; I give them silence. For the mind to flower it has to go beyond what it knows.

Q: Is the rhythm of your silence also the rhythm of the force of nature itself?

MM: It is the same. There is only one real rhythm; in silence you hear it. When you live to the rhythm of this silence, you become it, slowly; everything you do, you do to it.

Q: What is the relationship of your silence to my – or any devotee's – development?

MM: I do not speak but my force changes people completely. The power of the Divine works in the silence and will change things according to your aim and what you ask for. Sometimes I can give immediately what you have requested. Sometimes it takes time. Some people ask for each and every small thing, and others ask and go on asking – it depends on the individual. However, whether you ask or not is not important, I will give what is necessary.

Q: It seems that when we surrender to you we enter a great force field in which our reality is very quickly and dramatically transformed to show us what we need to understand. Would you say something about this?

MM: When you come into my presence or into connection with me your development speeds up and your karma becomes less. Because of my power, you can learn more in one life and can see more clearly and calmly so that understanding

No. 14
Thalheim, Germany 1984

comes easier. I give the Light to show you what you need to know. As you grow you will see your defects more clearly. This is due to the grace of the Divine.

Q: What is the best way to follow your inner teaching?

MM: Be like a child – clear, loving, spontaneous, infinitely flexible and ready each moment to wonder and accept miracle.

Q: The pain that comes on this path is very precise, isn't it?

MM: Yes. It lasts only as long as is necessary. My way is the way of joy; any pain that comes is to make you understand the nature of joy more deeply and bring you into joy.

Q: Sometimes I get an image of you burning away my soul.

MM: No. Your soul is always with me. I am burning the casing around your soul. The Light burns that so the soul can be free. You must desire the fire to stay and do its work. This desire makes the wood dry; if it is not dry it will take longer to become fire.

Q: How can I realize «Who am I?»

MM: Give up that 'I' and you will know.

Q: What daily discipline helps us realize the Divine?

MM: Remember the Divine in everything you do. If you have time, meditate. Offer everything to the Divine – everything good or bad, pure or impure. This is the best and quickest way.

Q: Is your method so simple because your power as an Avatar is so vast?

MM: Yes. Many people find that a complicated method is difficult to follow.

Q: Is our development much faster when we are devoted to an Avatar such as you?

MM: It depends on the level of devotion, but with an Avatar everything is possible.

Q: Does this yoga require a retreat from the world?

MM: Not at all. What is required is a synthesis and balance of the outer and inner lives.

Q: What is spirituality?

MM: To have spirituality is to love, aspire to, remember, surrender to the Divine. To have spirituality does not mean that one should not have a full life in the world. One should not leave the world – but the Divine should come first.

Q: How can one do God's work?

MM: In silence you give yourself to Him and He works through you. God is always working through you – the important thing is to become conscious and co-operate. This is done through surrender, love and the desire to serve with your whole being that springs from real love, and the knowledge of God's glory that the love of God brings. It can take a long time to learn how to give oneself, or it can take no time at all. It depends on the soul's ripeness.

Q: Could you describe a «ripe» devotee?

MM: When people are open and full of wordly and spiritual experience, they are ripe for realization and the merging in the Divine.

Q: Devotees who live around a great Master often think that they are the elect.

MM: Everyone here thinks that he or she is special. But to be special you have to know you are nothing.

Q: Could you describe the quality of trust toward the Divine that is needed in this yoga?

MM: Be simple. Be like a child. The child does not know where the mother is going but loves the mother and lets her carry him, knowing that the mother will never harm him.

Q: Some devotees say, «We do nothing; Mother does everything for us.» Is this the highest wisdom or just laziness?

MM: It is not the right way. It is a way of escaping what we have to do.

Q: In your book The Mother *you said, «Hurry, hurry. Awaken! Be conscious; come forward and help the world! The earth is waiting for the Light.» How can we hurry?*

MM: Be less concentrated on wordly life. Turn singlemindedly to God. Continue with your duties, but devote yourself entirely to God.

Q: How can we know if we will reach the Divine?

MM: Each person knows how much time he is devoting to the Divine and how much he surrenders.

Q: Can I reach the Divine through art or work?

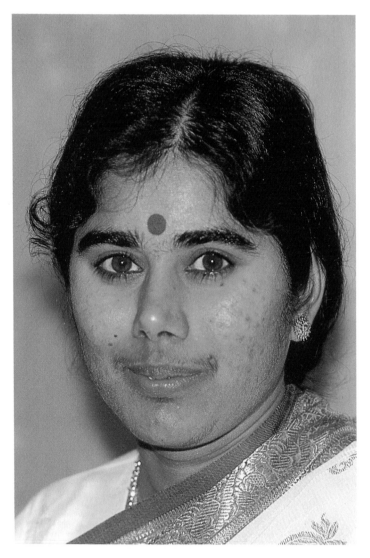

No. 24
Thalheim, Germany 1994

MM: Don't go to the Divine through anything – go directly. Realize yourself and see that everything you do is filled with Light. Don't live for your work only; live for Him and do your work in Him and for Him. If you surrender to Him truly, it will no longer be you who does the work but God who does it through you. You will become a channel for His power and His will and His Light. This takes time and a great purity of heart and motive.

Q: Would you describe the inner condition of someone who is spiritually open?

MM: To be open means to receive like a child – simply, with no constructions, no mind.

Open people are not rigid, they accept everything and have broad views. Spiritually open people automatically help others, no matter who they may be.

Open people may live in various ways. One may be content to have a family and make its members happy; another may leave his or her family and be a sannyasin; another may remain in the family but feel detached and so helps others also.

Q: Are there any bodily conditions – such as spine damage – that can block a spiritual opening?

MM: No physical defects can block a spiritual unfolding.

Q: What can we do to open further to the Mother?

MM: You have to pray wholeheartedly, do japa to divine personalities or a guru, and be sincere.

Q: How important is relaxation to spiritual opening?

MM: Being relaxed and peaceful is the most important thing for opening. When you are restless, you cannot open to the Divine.

Q: What is the importance of discipline in spiritual life?

MM: Having discipline helps in the development of the integral life – worldly, psychological, mental. It is easier to live in the world if we have discipline.

Q: How important is patience in your work?

MM: Patience is essential. If you are a gardener you know that once you have put a plant in, you have to respects the laws of nature and wait.

Q: To believe is not enough. Don't we have to KNOW?

MM: Belief is only the beginning. To be strong you must see. Then you can bear anything and do anything. Then the Work can be done simply. What is needed is the awareness of Unity at all moments. From that come love and truth and divine power.

Q: How do ethics relate to spiritual development?

MM: If you hate someone, you cannot grow, so you must change the hate into love. If you have negative feelings, you are not loving, and without love you cannot open to the Divine.

Q: Is curiosity an adequate reason to come to see you?

MM: Absolutely not. I want people to come because they are inspired from the heart to come, not because they are curious. This is serious work.

Q: Why do you have no rules for your devotees?

MM: What use is it telling people anything? Often they disagree and rebel. People must be strong in themselves. I say nothing but my Light changes people inwardly and helps them discover what they really want and need. The important thing is to pray and to receive Light. That in itself will change you.

When the heart opens to God, the rules follow. All people have their own rules for their own stage of understanding. What is necessary is to follow me inside. Then you will know what to do and how to act at all times.

Q: Do you expect your devotees to be a certain way?

MM: I want you to be completely yourself. Everyone is unique for me. Everyone grows in a different way, has different needs. I respect everyone as himself or herself. When you know that you are eternal you can play your true role in time. When you know you are divine you can become completely human. When you know you are one with God you are free to become absolutely yourself, individual and holy and my child.

THE RHYTHM OF THE PATH

Q: What are the stages of the path?

MM: It is better not to say – people may think wrongly that they are at one stage or another and may thereby delude themselves. As people grow, they will know how far they have come in their development. Their own experience will tell them how far they have reached and how far they still have to reach.

Q: Is there suffering at every stage of the path?

MM: In one way, yes. But joy becomes greater than pain. And pain becomes joy because it is offered and understood.

68

Q: It seems that a further stage of this yoga unfolds just when one thinks one is done.

MM: You must stop nowhere.

Q: The development on your path seems almost musical – with themes that return.

MM: In the end, you and reality will be one, one music, always changing and always the same. You will be playing yourself. I will be always tuning you.

Q: There is no end to real knowledge, is there, because there is no end to the journey into God?

MM: Yes, no end. One common mistake is to think that one reality is THE reality. You must always be prepared to leave one reality for a greater one.

TRADITIONAL PATHS AND THE WAY OF THE MOTHER

Q: All the Gods, all the paths, all the revelations are in the Mother. Does this mean that anyone in the world from whatever background can be taught by you and awakened to the Divine within the terms of their own religion or lack of it?

MM: Yes. My Light is everywhere.

Q: *Which is true, the Hindu sense of God as eternal presence or the Buddhist awareness of reality as emptiness?*

MM: Both are true – God is everything and nothing.

Q: *I believe in Jesus. Must I stop believing in him and believe in you?*

MM: Whomever you believe in, believe with all your heart. All divine incarnations are equal. Be sincere, open, and my help will be given to you always.

Q: *The Buddha taught that it was the doctrine itself that liberated and that a guru can only point the way. Can you, as an Avatar, give direct experience of God?*

MM: Yes.

Q: *How should a jnani or bhakta approach your path?*

MM: The jnani and bhakta approach the Divine in their own way; if they come to me, I will help and they can continue on their own path. As an Avatar, I have no special path, but come to give grace and power to those on all paths. Only in the sense that I give darshan do I have a path, but people of all paths can receive help from me whether or not they come to darshan.

Q: In the Hindu tradition, animals are not allowed in the puja room. What is your opinion on this matter?

MM: For the Divine there is no caste. Therefore, animals can come to the puja room. Sometimes animals open much better than humans. They can concentrate more fully because they don't have conceptual minds.

Q: Is it best to explore several paths and then choose one? What should one look for in choosing the most suitable path?

MM: Each person has his or her own path. Choose the one that is easy, convenient, and that comes spontaneously. The choice is influenced by one's past and by familiar practices.

DARSHAN

Q: Why is darshan performed so simply, without singing, for example?

MM: People are too active and rarely sit quietly. In silence one can receive more because all one's activities become concentrated at one point. My teaching is to give only the essence, the Divine, that which is necessary. I give exactly what is needed by each person.

Paramatman is silent. God is silent. Everything comes out of silence. In silence more work can be done. The true experience of bliss is without words.

Q: When we have your darshan we do pranam (bow down) in front of you and you take our heads between your hands: what are you doing?

MM: On the back of the human being is a white line running up from toes to the head. In fact, two lines start from the toes, rise along the legs, join at the base of the spine and then become a single line reaching to the top of the head. This line is thinner than a hair, and has some knots in it here and there which divine personalities help to undo. It is very delicate work and great care has to be taken to undo the knots, as there is danger for your life if the thread is broken. When I hold your head I am untying these knots. I am also removing other kinds of obstacles to your sadhana, your practice.

When I touch your head, the Light moves upwards in the white line. It indicates, like a meter, the development of your sadhana. When there is no progress, the Light moves downwards along the line, showing the degree to which your sadhana has deteriorated. When the Light is continuous from the toes to the top of the head, the person may have many experiences and visions, although some people have visions and experiences without this white line. When the line gets to the top of the head, people have the Paramatman darshan. When the line has gone above the head, then there is a constant relation with Paramatman.

If your aspiration weakens, the line moves downwards as I said. One day you might even fall from your sadhana. This is a great crisis, which can, however, be prevented. In the front of the body are two red lines starting from the toes, growing gradually upwards on either side of the legs and tending to meet at the base of the spine where the white lines become a single one. If the red lines reach the white line, you will achieve absolute detachment. This rarely happens and only to those who have the Divine Shakti.

By the growth of the white and red lines the sadhana will be established permanently without possibility of a fall. If the red lines develop fully, you will reach great heights. The white lines will also help to support the experiences of those who have a psychic opening. Even when there is a psychic opening there is still the possibility that it will close. The opening of the psychic is effective for sadhana, but it is not enough. The establishment of the white and red lines will help you to keep the psychic continually open. If the psychic can be compared to a flower, the lines are the plant itself.

Q: *When we have done pranam we look into your eyes in silence. What are you doing?*

MM: I am looking into every corner of your being. I am looking at everything within you to see where I can help, where I can give healing and power. At the same time, I am giving Light to every part of your being, I am opening every part of yourself to Light. When you are open you will feel and see this clearly.

Q: *What do you see when you look into people's eyes during darshan?*

MM: I see the difficulties in their lives and the obstacles to their sadhana.

Q: *How does the work that you do during pranam differ from that during darshan? Does it work on a different part of the being?*

MM: The work of each is different. During pranam the work is on the deep aspect of the being, the

B&W No. 3
Madanapalle, India 1993

soul, while darshan helps the personality and the life situation.

Q: In darshan, do you always use the Light to do your work, or do you also work in some other way?

MM: It is with the Light alone that my help comes.

Q: What parts of the human receive your Light?

MM: I give Light to the mental, vital, and physical bodies.

Q: I have the impression that when there are more people at darshan, there is also more Light and power. Why is this?

MM: Some people feel more Light when there are less persons and others feel the contrary. This is only according to their mentality. But the Light is the same always.

Q: You have spoken of working with the developing white and red lines in the body. Are these the same as or related to the sushumna, ida and pingala, and the development of the kundalini?

MM: They are different. In the kundalini system, one develops the chakras one at a time. But these lines help the whole being. When I undo the knots in them, this aids in the development of the entire

being, not just certain parts. Only divine personalities can see these lines – human beings cannot.
The lines are not related to the human personality;
they show the evolution of the soul itself.

Q: Is it necessary to awaken the kundalini?

MM: When the Light descends in the body it is not
necessary.

Q: Please describe the knots.

MM: Doubt would be an example of a knot. In this
case I would help clarify the doubt and give faith.

*Q: As I understand it, you do not untie the knots all at
once, but rather slowly. Does a devotee feel the effects of
the knots being loosened, or does he or she not feel the
results until the knots are completely untied?*

MM: The devotee can feel effects from the
loosening of the knots. The knots are loosened
slowly because to do so quickly could be dangerous.

*Q: Is it important to have many darshans to help loosen
the knots?*

MM: It does not depend on the number of
darshans. It depends on your sincerety, aspiration
and love.

Q: Is the process quickened by darshan?

MM: Yes, aspiration plus darshan is helpful.

Q: Is there any such thing as a bad or good darshan?

MM: There is no such thing as a bad darshan. To think so is wrong, harmful, and dangerous. Darshan is completely impersonal from my side; I give what is needed. Reactions depend upon the people who take, not the Mother who gives. Try not to impose on me your difficulties and to project on me your own hidden problems. Have the courage to face your own weaknesses and know that I am giving you help continually.

Q: In what way can I be most open during darshan?

MM: With silent mind and good concentration pray to the Divine to open you. If you can do this, you will feel the consequences of what I am giving to you. You won't receive more but you will feel it more.

Q: When it is my turn for pranam and darshan I have palpitations and erratic emotions. What can I do?

MM: Offer it all to the Divine. Be patient – these emotions will go.

Q: When we feel the force in darshan, how can we enter more deeply into it?

MM: The force will come and go on its own. You can pray that it returns and stays with you.

Q: How can I open to your energy as quickly as possible?

MM: People do not open «as quickly as possible». You must try, and I will help you. Be patient.

Q: How can we prepare ourselves to receive darshan?

MM: There is nothing special to do. In darshan one tries to sit silently with no thoughts. To do this one needs to be peaceful.

Q: You speak of sitting silently in darshan, with no thoughts. But I often pray. Is this all right?

MM: Silence means to sit physically quiet and to pray to God for the Divine and to do japa. Silence is a calm mind. It is better to sit silently than to leave immediately after darshan.

Q: Is there something special that we should try to do after darshan? Is there a way to prolong the blessing received during darshan?

MM: Be quiet. It is better not to rush out into another activity.

Q: Where did you learn the gestures of darshan?

MM: They came.

Q: Has anybody ever worked in the same way as you do?

MM: Each one has his or her own way of doing things. We cannot compare.

Q: Do you have discomfort in darshan?

MM: No, it is the best joy.

Q: Do you feel our pain, joy, and suffering in darshan?

MM: Yes.

Q: How can I thank you for what you are giving me?

MM: You are receiving. That is thanks. That is a great thing.

DARSHAN AT A DISTANCE

Q: How important is it to come to Thalheim to receive darshan from you?

MM: It is not necessary to come stay with me; I can help anywhere. People can come, but if this is not possible, it is unnecessary for them to become tense about it. The physical contact is one way of giving the Light, but it is not so important for me. However, when people come here, they feel the presence more concretely. With or without touch, we can get the Light.

Q: Some people who live far away cannot come for pranam and darshan. Can your work on them be done at a distance?

MM: Yes, if there is sincerity.

Q: Can even the physical be transformed at a distance, without the physical touch?

MM: Yes, it is possible.

Q: When devotees are far away, can you see the state of their red and white lines, and do you continue to loosen the knots at a distance? Is pranam necessary for this work?

MM: I can see the red and white lines from far away and can loosen the knots wherever the devotees are. As long as there is aspiration, the work can be done. But when the devotees are here they feel the presence strongly and this helps them.

Q: Does your force need your directed attention in order for it to work?

MM: No, it works automatically; the Light works by itself.

Q: I dreamed I received your darshan. Do you give darshan at night?

MM: I am giving darshan always, everywhere.

INNER CONTACT

Q: What should we do to receive your Light and help when you are not with us physically? How can we find the constant inner contact with you? What should we do to progress in our practice, our sadhana? Do you expect anything from those who put in your hands the direction of their life and their sadhana?

MM: Concerning sadhana, you must do japa when you want to receive my Light and help when I am not physically with you. Only through japa do you have constant inner contact with me. If you want to make any progress in the sadhana, you must practice japa. This is the easy way to remember the Divine. I do not expect anything from any human beings, but when they are sincere and serious in their sadhana, it gives me happiness.

Q: Most people who come to you see you only in darshan. What is the best relationship that they can then develop with you?

MM: The best way to be near me is to remember me. Similarly, to remember the Divine brings the presence. Love, sincerity, and aspiration connect us to the Divine.

Q: Although I live far away from you, yet I feel your presence strongly and concretely. Is it true or simply imagination?

MM: It is true. Those who have real aspiration for the Divine, wherever they may be in the world, will receive my help and my Light. As a result, their realization will go faster.

Q: During the day, when we feel the pressure of your presence – in the heart chakra or the head, for example – should we stop what we are doing and pay immediate attention to it?

MM: The presence comes and goes by itself. If possible you can stop your activity to concentrate on it, but whether or not you pay attention to it, it will do as it will. You can aspire for it to come more often.

Q: Could you describe the relation of your mind to that of the devotee?

MM: When the devotee has doubts, I give Light to the mind to see things clearly. This is an ordinary and simple thing for me to do. It is not that I read his or her mind, but when something is not clear, I will make it clearer.

Q: How do you know the condition of a person at some distance away?

MM: I see.

Q: Is a photo of Mother useful?

Adilakshmi: Yes, the picture of Mother is not simply a picture. Part of the Divine is there. Mother's power is there. You are actually seeing Mother when you look at the picture.

Q: What is the best way to communicate with you?

MM: The soul connection is best, it is best to feel it inside – but you can also write.

Q: How best can we follow your inner teachings?

MM: When you become aware that there is something you need to understand, ask me inwardly, quite simply, with love and surrender, and I will teach it to you.

Q: When you are no longer in the body will people be able to pray to you and connect with you?

MM: Yes, always.

Q: Some people say they hear your voice interiorly, in their minds, guiding them. Is it truly you who speaks?

MM: Usually not. I recommend that people neither pay attention to nor determine their actions on the basis of such voices, as it is difficult to tell where these voices come from. However, when devotees are in extreme situations – danger, for example – the guiding voice they hear is more likely to be my own.

Q: Should we listen to an inner voice that warns us when we are making, or about to make, a wrong movement?

MM: It is not always good to follow the inner voice. One must also look at the circumstances and use common sense.

Q: I have the feeling that you send messages to me through X.

MM: Yes, it is often like that – that other people deliver the words that a devotee needs to hear.

B&W No. 4
Essen, Germany 1981

Q: I feel that you are ripening me, inspiring everything in my development. Is it so?

MM: You are letting it happen. That is a great thing. I can give everything but you must want everything. I can give many things even before you know you want them, but when you know it is quicker and more joyful.

Q: Could you give me a symbol?

MM: Isn't the joy in your heart symbol enough?

MEDITATION/JAPA

Q: Is formal meditation important?

MM: Yes, to meditate a half an hour or an hour is good. But if one becomes fanatical, wants to leave one's job, live alone and meditate twenty-four hours a day, that is not good.

Q: What kind of meditation should we do?

MM: Close your eyes and sit in silence and do japa on any divine name.

Q: What is japa? Why is it so important?

MM: Japa is the repetition of the name of that in which we believe. Japa is essential. Japa is not simple words – each divine name is full of divine vibrations. These surround us and protect us and penetrate both our bodies and our whole inner being. Remembrance of the divine name gives immediate peace and happiness and turns us from the wordly to the Divine. There is no special and limited time for japa. It is very good to do japa all day. If this is not possible then remember whenever it is possible. We can practice japa during all activities. It is easier to remember when we do physical work without mental work. This japa helps us to purify our consciousness and make our sadhana easy.

Q: How should we say japa?

MM: Simply. Just say it. In doing japa, one should not strain or try to achieve something specific. One should try to be sincere and to have love of God. The power immediately follows, whether you are aware of it or not.

Q: Would you explain the power of the name?

MM: Each syllable of a divine name – such as Krishna or Jesus – has vibrations which change the atmosphere. Any object that we think about repeatedly generates its own vibration. Even though mantras are strong and powerful, we may not feel the effects immediately but results will come. One can feel the differences in the vibrations of words. Using the word, one can make things change.

Q: Is it necessary to wait for a guru to give a mantra or may one find a mantra on one's own?

MM: Whichever mantra comes to you easily and spontaneously is the one you should do. It should give a strong feeling and be like music flowing from the heart.

Q: I don't have a fixed japa. At different times different forms of the Divine – such as Shiva or Krishna – come into my mind, and I sing the appropriate mantra. Is doing this all right?

MM: Yes, whatever appeals at the moment is all right. One doesn't have to have a fixed mantra.

Q: When I repeat your name is it necessary to say the mantra as given in The Mother, *or can I just repeat* Mother Meera *or simply* Meera?

MM: Either is sufficient.

Q: In meditation on a form of the Divine, is it enough to just have the feeling of the Divine, or must one say the mantra as well?

MM: It is enough to have the feeling. But it is good to mentally repeat the name of the Divine as well, because doing this trains the mind and heart.

Q: What are the different stages of meditation?

MM: When you first try to meditate, thoughts come. Then they cool down. Next you see some visions. Then the mind becomes empty. Some people think that there is nothing there and stop meditating. But if you continue you will finally realize.

Q: Does everyone have visions at some point?

MM: Most people will, but a few will not.

Q: What is the best technique of meditation?

MM: There are so many techniques. Generally they confuse people. Quite often they increase people's spiritual pride instead of destroying it. The proud man is far from God. You have to be very careful. The best way is to remember the Divine in everything and to offer everything to the Divine.

Q: Is there something we can do to transform our dream and sleep states so that they become more a part of our practice?

MM: If we practice japa while we are awake, this can carry over into the dream state. We can pray to the Divine for help in this.

Q: What do you think of the practice, used in many religions, of thinking that oneself is God?

MM: To say «I am God» is not good. Only when we merge in the Divine can we say this. As long as we have our own thoughts, feelings, desires, then it is not right.

Q: Sometimes I imagine my cells or my heart opening to the Light. Are such imaginings helpful?

MM: No. It is better to be silent. Through practicing such imaginations you are building illusions and may find yourself in an illusory world. It is better to go directly for the essence. Some people who imagine that they are divine get obsessive delusions that they are God. Then they may act aloof and stop working and so forth. It is healthier to keep one's devotion to God. Particularly during the Kali Yuga, this present age, it is better for most people to keep the dualistic standpoint – devotion to the Divine. Then, at the highest level, advaita (non-dualism) naturally comes.

SPIRITUAL EXPERIENCES

Q: In your yoga, one says japa, concentrates on the Divine, and tries to clear the mind as much as possible so as to be receptive to the Light and its work. When experiences start to come, is there any map we can follow?

MM: Experiences will come and will go. Sometimes devotees ask my opinion of an experience, but do not listen to my advice if it does not feed their egotism. It is not useful to think about whether experiences are real or unreal. Even by thinking, you cannot determine whether they are true or not. Whatever experiences come, great or small, it is better to offer them to the Divine and to continue doing japa. Otherwise your concentration will be on the experience and not on the Divine.

Q: How am I to understand the mystical experiences that I have?

MM: The answers and directions will come. The mind has to be prepared first. The experiences will happen and the Light will prepare the mind to understand the experiences.

Q: Should people be silent about their experiences?

MM: Whether or not to tell our experiences depends on the hearers, their level of interest and depth of understanding. It is of no use speaking of experiences to those who are not interested.

Q: When you appear in a dream, are you really there?

MM: It depends on the circumstances of the dream.

Q: How can I tell which visions come from the Divine and which come from my own fantasy?

MM: It is difficult sometimes. People like to make up things, and the mind is very clever. The visions that come from the Divine change you. They make you more loving and more humble. And more proud in the good way, proud of the Divine.

Q: Can a visionary experience of being God lead to power-madness?

MM: Not if the vision is real. If the vision is real you see the greatness of God. A real vision brings adoration of the Divine, and in that adoration there can be no vanity.

Visions are helpful, and you must be grateful for them. They are signs, they deepen faith, they show you what you must aim for. But the real work is in building love and silence, in changing your whole character and mind. Visions come and go. The silence remains. The silence brings continual connection, continual presence.

Q: As we awaken we realize that we are part of the Divine, not the whole Divine. This realization curtails any pride, doesn't it?

MM: If there is pride or vanity, then you are not awake. The really great saints and yogis are always the most humble. Humility is love; humility is what the heart knows. True joy is humble, because it is pure and given. A humble man is always quick to see his mistakes. Unless you are humble, the Divine will not use you. My power will only pass through you when you are clear – otherwise it would be dangerous for you. You must keep yourself clear at all times. The ego will keep on trying to seize for itself what the soul is learning.

Q: Sometimes, when I have had big experiences, I wonder if I am mad.

MM: If you must be mad, be mad in a good way – mad with divine love.

Q: What is the third eye, what does it see? At what stage does it open?

MM: This eye comprehends all things. It sees the whole picture – for example, it can see the background to the actions of others. At what stage it opens varies with the individual. It is not intuitive; it SEES everything clearly.

Q: What is samadhi like?

MM: People in real samadhi are above the five elements and do not need food, air, and water. They are blissful, powerful, and complete in themselves. For those who have attained samadhi it is easy to reach realization.

Q: Is the attainment of samadhi necessary for realization of God?

MM: No. It is only one way, one path, the jnana path. In the bhakti path we can realize the Divine with love. With a successful family life we can realize, with the devotion of Mirabai we can realize. Anasuya worshipped her husband, a saint, as divine and became realized.

Q: What is an appropriate attitude to have towards one's spiritual experiences?

MM: First, be grateful. Offer them to Him who sent them. He gave them to you, give them back to Him in love. Never think that you are special or chosen.

Know that if you do, it is the ego that is thinking these things. The very thing that these experiences are trying to overcome can use them. The ego is clever, it can use even the experience of the Divine.

Remember that however extraordinary the experiences, there are always further and greater experiences. The mind is finite but the spirit is infinite. There is no limit to transformation. The transformation I am doing is within the being and power of God and so limitless by nature.

There are many ways in which the mental and vital powers can imitate and pervert the spiritual. It takes time to become aware of how these different powers work. It is hard sometimes to tell where exactly an experience comes from. This is where discipline is necessary, and purification, and the grace of the Mother.

PRAYER

Q: What is the importance of asking the Divine for something?

MM: If you want anything – love, truth, or courage, for example – you must ask for it. If you ask God for anything humbly and lovingly, you will

No. 10
Thalheim, Germany 1984

receive it. But you must ask with your whole heart, so that your heart can be empty and God can fill it. If there is any pride in it, he cannot fill it as much. God wants to give you everything; you must learn how to let him. For this you need surrender. The reward of surrender is bliss and knowledge.

Q: What should I ask you for?

MM: Ask for everything – like a child asks its mother for everything, without shame. Do not stop at peace of mind or purity of heart or surrender. Demand everything. Don't be satisfied with anything less than everything. If you ask, you will receive. If you receive, you will have to bear.

Q: What is the relationship of karma and prayer? What is the use of prayer if all that happens is according to our karma?

MM: If we only accept our karma and act according to that, there will be no end to it – our karma will continue for many, many lives. However, if we pray and offer the fruits of our actions to the Divine, then our karma can be stopped, lessened, or transformed.

Q: How do you work with a person's karma? How are hindrances removed?

MM: Some karmas can be removed but others are very big and cannot be removed. However, in these cases, I can help people to dwell less and less on their problems and thus greatly reduce the pain. If we believe in God, when difficulties come in ordinary life we do not feel them so strongly and can pass through them with a light heart. Thinking about problems too much only makes them worse, and even a little problem can lead to a big explosion in the end. As to how hindrances are removed, there are no words to describe this.

Q: Do all people have their own protective angels?

MM: There are different angels for different purposes – they only come when needed.

Q: When we are having problems, does writing to you help? Is praying enough?

MM: Those devotees with much heart always want to write, whatever the problem. They always turn to the Mother. Some other devotees, with much mind, do not want to write because they are afraid of my having a record of their problems, which they want to keep hidden. In general, people should write with their problems, and then they will get direct help. Though some people can receive answers directly through prayer, the prayers of many others may not be deeply sincere and thus they do not receive help so quickly. Many people delay in writing about their problems, but when they finally do write and mail their letters, they may get an answer immediately, long before I receive the letter. Each person must decide for himself or herself whether or not to write.

Q: Is there a need for an intermediary in prayer? Sometimes it seems difficult to pray to God directly.

MM: Those who pray to Paramatman directly have a strong belief in Paramatman. Because they have confidence that God will help them, they do not go to intermediaries. Whether there are intermediaries or not, in the end all prayers go to Paramatman.

Q: Does grace come from you directly to us or through the intermediary of our own atman, our soul?

MM: Grace comes directly, there is no intermediary. God is always helping us.

Q: Can average people effectively pray for others, even though we are so small?

MM: However small we may be, it is helpful to ask Paramatman to remove our obstacles and those of others. Prayer always helps. In the eyes of Paramatman we are always small children.

Q: In certain spiritual traditions, one way of helping others is to hold up their image calmly in the silence of deep meditation. Are techniques such as this helpful, and are there others that you could recommend?

MM: It is better simply to pray and ask the Divine directly to help others and protect them.

Q: When a friend is going through difficulty, and words don't help, what can we do?

MM: Just pray silently for the person. This is the most helpful thing one can do.

Q: When we feel your energy strongly, is it helpful to direct it to others who need help?

MM: You cannot transmit the Light to others. The Light that comes to you is helpful only for you.

Q: Can we help others to be enlightened?

MM: Prayer for others is useful for this, and it helps us as well to remember the Divine.

Q: It is difficult to find time to pray during the day.

MM: It is not difficult; it is a question of making a habit of prayer.

Q: Is it possible to talk to God?

MM: When we offer everything to God, we will know He heard because results come. Someday, when we are ripe, we will directly hear the voice of God.

LOVE AND DEVOTION

Q: Why is devotion to the Divine important?

MM: If you have devotion you will get everything.

Q: How does one grow in devotion?

MM: One should have sincere aspiration to develop devotion and pray sincerely to the Divine.

Q: Sometimes I weep for God. Is this good?

MM: Mr. Reddy used to say often how strange it was that men would weep for the loss of money or a woman but not spend one sleepless night praying to God. Ramakrishna used to say that also. Look how much he wept and prayed for the Divine Mother. It is a great thing to weep for God. How often do people weep for a lover who then throws them away! But God remembers every small prayer, every tear. A tear is a door through which I can come. How can I come into a heart that doesn't long for me?

Why should people feel it is a shameful thing to weep for God? Look at Krishna's gopis; look at Mirabai. You must love greatly to desire the great love of God. You must leave all other loves for this one. Yet to do this you have to know the value of the Divine. Many lives can go past without one taste of divine bliss. If you do not want to waste this life, the holy desire for God is essential.

Q: Does one ever give up the desire for God?

MM: Even the Avatar has to desire to be in God at every moment. And when the Avatar dies, he desires with all his or her being to be united with God. Realization is the beginning of the true desire for an ever deeper Union.

Q: God is formless. But in order to love the Divine, isn't it necessary to love one of the formed aspects of God – Krishna or Jesus, for example?

MM: One can love the Divine directly and also through gods, angels, and gurus.

Q: How should we practice bhakti, devotion?

MM: It is not necessary to offer flowers and incense. Whatever you do can be offered without expectation of return. Love your master with sincerity and surrender.

Q: How are the paths of jnana and bhakti related to each other?

MM: To be a jnani is to know, and the more that you know the Divine, the more you love. To be a bhakti is to choose the path of love, and the more you love the Divine, the more you know.

Q: Sometimes we have concentration for the Divine, but sometimes we are attached to other matters.

MM: When you think that you are not thinking enough of the Divine, this is aspiration which also goes to the Divine.

Q: I do not always have a genuine feeling of love and devotion for the Divine.

MM: To remember the Divine, even if it is only done with the mental, will lead one to the experience of the Divine.

Q: I feel rejected by God sometimes.

MM: When we don't feel the love of God, we feel His absence as a punishment. When we feel the love of God we wonder how we did not feel it before.

Q: What is your opinion of atheism?

MM: There are no atheists. Everyone is devoted to something – whether it is called art or anything else.

Q: What is the difference between our genuine need for the Mother and our sincere love for her?

MM: These are different. When we need, this is for ourself. When we love her, we have no expectation of anything.

Q: Is it a problem for a devotee to love you personally as well as to love the Divine in you?

MM: If you are fixed on my outer personality and outer form, conflict and disappointment can arise. But if your inner relation to me is good, then all is well.

Q: When we begin to feel the extraordinary intensity of your love for us, does this mean we are beginning to return it?

MM: There is only one love and one energy. When you are feeling it, you are beginning to understand it.

Q: How does bhakti become non-dual?

MM: Duality exists until we merge in the Divine; then there is only the One. As love grows toward the master we merge gradually in the Divine. The process goes slowly so that we can have a growing taste of the Divine. If it doesn't go slowly then the body cannot feel it. If we don't feel it then the devotion we need for our transformation doesn't grow. When we get complete realization then every aspect of us goes into the Divine.

SURRENDER AND OFFERING

Q: By teaching in silence and by bringing down the force of the Paramatman Light you are asking for a very deep and very intense surrender. Would you help us to understand clearly what surrender is?

MM: To offer everything to the Divine is surrender. To give our lives to the Divine is surrender. Simplicity is surrender. When we are simple the ego will dissolve by itself; when we are simple the answers will come. Always to remember, no matter how great we are, that there is something greater – the Divine – is surrender. Not to be egoistic is surrender. To be humble is surrender.

Q: What is surrender?

MM: To surrender is to offer whatever you do to the Divine and to follow scrupulously what the wise tell you. One important form of surrender is to live by the rules of whatever religion you choose.

Q: Isn't «surrendering» being weak?

MM: No. Real surrender is not weakness. It is the strongest thing a man can do. You have to be strong to give away everything.

Q: Why should one offer everything to the Divine?

MM: Offering everything, pure and impure, is the best and quickest way to develop spiritually. If you offer everything to the Divine, the Divine will accept and change it, even the worst things. It is not what you offer but THAT you offer which is important. Offer everything, and you will acquire the habit of thinking always about God. THAT will change you.

Q: What is offering?

MM: Loving politeness. Whatever you do, give it to God with a grateful and humble heart.

Q: How does one offer something to God?

MM: We can say that we are offering something to God in whatever way we want – by using words or by just feeling it. If we want to offer something

No. 16
Thalheim, Germany 1993

good, we can simply thank God for it. With negative things, we can offer them to God and ask God to take them away. Or by simply offering them, we can come to feel embarrassed by what we are giving to God, and so begin to change.

Q: May we enjoy the material life?

MM: You may enjoy the material life, but offer it to the Divine.

Q: What does it mean when Krishna tells Arjuna in the Bhagavad Gita to give up the fruits of all actions?

MM: If you think, «I do this action,» you become egotistic. Instead of being egotistic, offer everything to the Divine. If you offer everything to the Divine, there is no ego. If there is no ego you become divine.

Q: How does one develop aspiration?

MM: Offer everything you do to the Divine and this will develop aspiration.

Q: Many devotees bring flowers and presents. What is the best thing we can offer to you? Is it also our dark ego movements?

MM: Yes, especially the ego. And your joy. What-ever you offer should be offered sincerely, not as a duty.

Q: But the ego is horrible.

MM: Nothing is horrible for the Divine.

Q: Is the nature of the offering to the Divine important?

MM: A child brings its mother a marble, a snail, a stick. The mother doesn't look at the gift. She is happy the child thought of her. What is any gift to God? God has everything. You are only giving back to God what he gave to you. The gift is not important, only the love.

THE EGO

Q: How does the ego arise?

MM: The body, vital, and especially the mind thinking they are the self brings in egoism.

Q: How does the ego block the truth force when it is so weak?

MM: Compared to the Divine the ego is weak, but in the world, it is strong.

Q: Why do people take the world as real?

MM: Because they concentrate on things, and see diversity rather than unity.

Q: In the world the ego is strong – how do we get away from the ego without running from the world?

MM: If you grow inside, the ego will drop. Meditation, japa, and prayer weaken the ego.

Q: Must the dismantling of the ego always feel like a death?

MM: To achieve realization a dying to the old self, the ego, is necessary. But why be sad about it? What has the old self given you that you should love it so? The divine self will give you all things and also give you bliss. Do not think in terms of «giving up» anything. Think of «growing». Think of always growing stronger and more loving and more complete. Then what you wanted yesterday you will not want today and what you wanted today tomorrow you will see is not useful. Discipline must be there, and control – not in the name of «death», but in the name of love and true life. You have to cut a tree sometimes to make it straight and help it grow.

Q: Is the death of the ego necessary?

MM: For God no ego is necessary. To live in this world the ego is necessary. You can choose.

PAIN ON THE PATH

Q: What should people do with the fear that comes in the process of spiritual unfolding?

MM: They should not be afraid of it. It is common and natural; it cannot be stopped. But it will go. As joy will come and go, so will fear. Accept this simply, and go on.

Q: How should I deal with that fear that sometimes arises?

MM: Why grieve or be afraid? Go deeper into joy. Work with joy. That is the way to end grief and fear.

Q: What should I do about the despair I feel when I fail?

MM: Failing is not important. Everyone will fail for some time. Everyone will make mistakes. But you must not be discouraged. You must never think, «I cannot do this.» You must know it is not you that is doing the work; it is the Mother. You must have faith in her. Of course you must work too – but in a peaceful way, with an open heart.

Q: My mind is always creating difficulties. What should I do?

MM: Try to be wise enough to know that you do not know. Then the Divine can lead you forward into true knowledge, calmly, stage by stage. Give me your mind without fear and I will expand it. When the heart suffers, it is easy to transform its suffering into joy, but when the mind creates and lives a fantasy, it is extremely hard to change it. So be very careful. Do not let your mind become your worst enemy.

Q: Sometimes I feel like giving up hope.

MM: At no moment should a man give up hope. If he gives up hope he is killing himself. There is always hope.

Q: But a man must be humble to hope.

MM: He must know himself. That will make him humble. Then he can have true hope.

Q: Why is it that after people experience some measure of your Light they are later confronted with negative moods and strong desires?

MM: Emotions such as anger do not arise in order to block our progress. They are there, within us, and cannot always be controlled. They must come out so that we can understand them and offer them to the Divine. All that is inside will come out. Even with developed people emotions such as anger arise, but the quality of the anger changes, although the quantity may remain the same. These emotions remain until we merge with Param-atman.

Q: Why must our weaknesses and faults come into focus so clearly just when we are trying so hard to emphasize the «shinier» sides of our personalities?

MM: In order to do my work, people must know their bad points. And they must know these completely so that they are not their own victims. The Force can work only through the humble. You must know the difference between the human and the Divine in you, so you can transform the human BY the Divine.

Q: In spite of everything I have experienced with you, I still sometimes doubt you.

MM: Doubt is useful. It keeps you honest. Sometimes people say how much they love me and love God, but I know what is in their hearts. It is better when someone says, «I love you», knowing all the hatred and doubt that is still within them. Then it means something. Then the love can grow. Whatever doubts come, however frightening they are, know they are the creation of your mind. Only the Light is real. It is difficult for the ego to accept this.

But do not be ashamed of doubt. You are human, and these things come to the human being. Use every energy to change yourself. There is only one energy and when you know that, you can turn every impulse towards me, offer everything up, however bad you think it is, to be transformed.

SUFFERING

Q: Religions such as Christianity and Buddhism take the view that suffering is good in so far as it drives us to seek God. Does suffering have a role in sadhana?

MM: Suffering is one way, but not the main way. It comes by itself; you don't have to ask for it. If you are suffering, naturally you will ask for happiness. But the Divine never says that suffering is necessary – this idea is created by human beings. The Divine asks us to be happy, harmonious and peaceful.

Q: How does suffering work to bring about change?

MM: People suffer a great deal in life without knowing why. When there is Grace, you are helped to know why and to change. The greatest pain is ignorance. When the pain is clear, you can find its source and can change.

Q: What is your attitude to suffering in the body?

MM: Pain belongs to the body, so it must be accepted.

Q: Can we alleviate our own suffering?

MM: When we are insincere we feel suffering. When we are sincere there is no suffering – we are concentrating on the Mother so that even if we have physical suffering we will not feel it. We cannot say that there is no pain at all, but as we do not feel that it belongs to us it is weakened. If we have faith we feel less pain.

How we consider suffering depends on our mentality. When we offer pain to the Divine we are free of it. Focusing on the pain only increases it. Humans make the pain more than it is by concentrating on it.

Q: Why did the Divine create the world in this way so that there is pain?

B&W No. 5   Mr. Reddy and Mother Meera. Pondicherry, India 1978

MM: By their mental creations humans magnify the small pain that is in the world into a big drama.

INTELLECT

Adilakshmi: How many times I have seen it! People come in here with so many questions but just sitting with Ma sweeps everything from their minds. They come with questions and they go away with peace. The peace and joy are the answer.

Q: Can language convey the truth?

MM: Language can point to the truth.

Q: What is the importance of understanding philosophic systems?

MM: Studying different paths is useful because it gives a knowledge of the path in general as well as a respect for other traditions. If we know only a few paths we may hold a limited, rigid view. A broad background is better – it helps us when we have experiences by giving us clarification and confidence that we are going in the right direction.

Q: Which teacher's writings do you especially recommend?

MM: Each religion has its basic books. It is helpful to read these fundamental works of any religion. Of course we can read other books that appeal, but the basic things we must know. Read the works of many sages and saints, not just one, in order to get a variety of views.

Q: I have noticed that I find out what I need to know only at the moment when I am strong enough to bear that knowledge.

MM: Yes. There is no use in knowing things before you are ready. That way leads to confusion.

Q: Should we try to curb the use of the intellect?

MM: If the mind does not disturb or destroy others, then it can go on doing what it may.

Q: The clarity that I need in order to do your work, is it of the mind?

MM: The clarity is of the spirit, of the Light. But the mind is useful. Train it to be awake. Train it to be lit up with the spirit. Make it a servant and not a master. There is great joy for the mind in following the spirit.

REALIZATION

Q: Can we regard Paramatman as the Self?

MM: Only when you merge with Paramatman.

Q: What is the atman, the soul?

MM: The atman comes from the Paramatman. Just as the atman is essential for the body so is Paramatman important for the atman. The atman guides our development and is the basis or root cause of all our physical and subtle bodies. It works through all the various bodies to experience everything and then will take all this experience back to Paramatman in realization.

Q: What is our relationship to the soul?

MM: The soul acts as a protector during our lives, and is always with us. It has no wishes of its own. It is not only a witness or a guide but also helps our development. Free from the influence of our actions, it remains permanently with us through our lives until we unite with the Divine.

Q: Is it the atman that is ignorant of its divine origin?

MM: The atman has no desires and is free from suffering. It comes from Paramatman and has the qualities of the Light. It is not the atman that becomes realized.

Q: What is the process of realization?

MM: The body, vital, and mind must learn how to cooperate with the atman. When we have experienced everything we need to experience, the atman with all the sheaths can merge into Paramatman.

Q: If in meditation I could quiet the mind, would there be a realization of the atman?

MM: The mind and the vital gradually change and understand more, before realization occurs.

Q: When people claim to realize God are they really realizing the atman?

MM: Many people say they have realized. Some people say they have realized in order to avoid ordinary obligations. The truly realized do not say they have realized. Realization of the soul is not full realization. What I mean by realization is realization of Paramatman, not the atman.

Q: When we realize God, is it only part of God or all of God?

MM: Realization is of the total Godhead, not a part.

Q: Can one get liberation in one life?

MM: It takes many lives and hard spiritual practice. It is not good to think too much of realization. Do the practice for the sake of the Divine, not for the sake of liberation.

Q: Could you describe realization? Some people think that the realized person becomes like a stone, without feeling.

MM: Realization is absolute feeling, absolute freedom to love everything and to know everything. It is the unrealized man who is like a stone; the realized man is like a bird, all life and true energy and beauty.

Q: What is a realized man like?

MM: Like a child at peace in the womb of the Mother, knowing he is sustained at every moment by the grace and Light of the Divine Mother.

Q: Do all the descriptions of enlightenment in various religions refer to the same thing?

MM: The different religions may use various techniques, but in the end they reach the same goal.

Q: What is sahaja?

MM: Ordinarily, humans always differentiate where God is and is not – in sahaja you will experience everything as God.

Q: Is there one moment when a person becomes realized?

MM: There are many awakenings in the process. But there is no end to realization. You must always remember that you are traveling forward, and be attached to nothing. There is no end to the journey. The good qualities of the mind can be endlessly expanded. You must open more and more, always become more and more loving, more and more peaceful, more and more balanced, more and more harmonious.

Q: What is complete realization?

MM: To merge into Paramatman is complete realization. You can realize Paramatman without merging, while still embodied. But complete realization happens after death when you no longer have a body; merging is the end of all lives – you never come back. Although there are a few special exceptions, it is usual for most beings to merge and not return.

B&W No. 6
Pondicherry, India 1979

Q: What happens to all this development of the bodies when we merge with Paramatman? Is it of no further use?

MM: Yes, unless Paramatman sends you back for a special task. Then that development is of use. At the moment of death, the realized person can choose not to merge but to return to help others.

Q: In the Buddhist mahayana path, there is the strong wish to become a buddha for the sake of others and to return to help them. What do you think about this?

MM: Merging into the Divine is essential. After that, everything is Paramatman, we do not exist further and only do the bidding of Paramatman. If Paramatman should ask us to return, then we will. We have no wish of our own.

Q: I read in a book that one can realize the Divine within an hour.

MM: With divine grace one can realize the Divine within a second.

WORKING IN THE WORLD

Q: What is the best way to live?

MM: It doesn't matter how you live – you can lead a normal life. It is not necessary to consecrate your whole life to the Divine. But whatever you do, try to remember the Divine as much as possible. Your only aim should be to aspire always for God.

Q: Do I have to leave my job and family to do your work?

MM: No. Sadhana can be done within family life. People should stay where they are and turn all their attention to the Divine and open to the Light. That is everything. You don't have to be near me physically to do my work. Wherever you are, if your aspiration is sincere, I shall be with you.

Q: I would prefer not to be in the world at all, but rather spend my time meditating. What do you think?

MM: In general I recommend a balance between wordly life and spiritual life. One must love the world and its people, not feel a repulsion for them. There is nothing wrong with the world – the Divine is everywhere. It is just that usually we are not good enough truly to see the world.

Q: Couldn't I retreat from the world and live on a government subsidy?

MM: It is not good to live on someone else's money. You accrue karma.

Q: But if I only get a small amount from the government?

MM: Karma is karma, nothing to do with little or smaller or greater or more.

Q: I can't live in the world and follow you.

MM: You must learn to bear both worlds.

Q: Isn't it best to find a situation in which one need not work so as to devote oneself full time to spiritual matters?

MM: I do not accept that people do not work. Everyone must work. I am working. Everyone must do what they can. This is not a time for people to withdraw from the world. It is a time to work with the power and love of the Divine IN the world. I don't accept people of any age just coming here to be with me. I want people to come and go. When people are really dedicated to the Divine, there is no difference between action and prayer.

Q: Do you recommend ashram life?

MM: No, I am not interested in ashrams. I am not interested in founding a movement for people who do not want to work, who want only to sit around and think about what they think is God. People should go on living their ordinary lives. Family life is a very good place to do my work. It teaches people to be unselfish. I want people to be strong, self-reliant, unselfish, and to contribute to the world with whatever skills and gifts they have. I want them to work. All the old separations between «holy» and «wordly» are not real. Everything is divine. Everything. All this is God. Everyone must become conscious of this.

Q: Some people think that intellectual work is more dignified than hand-work, that spiritual work is one thing and wordly work another.

MM: This is not true. There is no difference. For me there is no difference between any of the forms of work.

Q: Do you recommend retreats to practice japa and other meditations?

MM: The Divine is everywhere. It is not necessary to go on retreat. But there is no rigid rule about this – if someone desires to go that is all right.

134

Q: Isn't the important thing not just to do one's work, but to do it as part of our sadhana and with the same care?

MM: Yes, you have to give the same importance to your work and sadhana, and then balance these.

Q: If I concentrate too strongly on the Divine while I am working, won't I lose contact with the work and be inefficient?

MM: No. If one thinks of the Divine, the work happens more spontaneously and harmoniously. If one approaches work with the mind only, many things can go wrong.

Q: Is it selfish to be concerned with our spiritual life or should we try to help others?

MM: To help others is always best. But balance and synthesis is important. Don't concentrate in only one direction.

Q: What is the perfect life?

MM: To realize the Divine is the only perfect life.

HUMAN RELATIONSHIPS

Q: What is love?

MM: To go on doing for people what they need, without expecting anything in return, that is love.

Q: Is human love part of divine love?

MM: No love comes without divine grace.

Q: When people fall in love, they often feel that their love flows out to all people. Is this helpful spiritually?

MM: Falling in love and experiencing this greater lovingness is helpful in terms of living in the world, but should not be confused with spirituality. The capacity to love many humans does not necessarily mean that you will more easily love the Divine. But falling in love is not bad – some people become grateful to the Divine for this experience. But others just forget the Divine.

Q: Is even the deepest human love an attachment?

MM: To love a human being is an attachment; to love the Divine is also an attachment. Love is love. If we know how to love, we can love each other and may also love the Divine. Love comes spontaneously and has no rules and regulations; it should be allowed to grow.

It is not compulsory to love me. If you love another, the love will come to me.

Q: Does love for one's family lead to love of God?

MM: If a man learns to love his wife and child properly, he will learn the habit of love, he will learn to begin to be selfless. Then he can turn his heart to God.

Q: What is the spiritual importance of family life?

MM: A calm and harmonious family is a great spiritual achievement, as is a true marriage. It takes much work and sacrifice from everyone. The world is a family. True perception is to see oneself as part of this family and to see everyone as related to you, a part of yourself. This perception is what the real monk and sannyasin are working for also. If they retreat from family life it should be to find the world a family. Otherwise their search is selfish, not enlightened.

Q: Is it easier for a single person to do sadhana?

MM: It is not a question of whether or not you are married, but of whether or not you are sincere. If two people in a relationship are really focused on the Divine and are right for each other, their progress can even be faster than that of a single person, because they complement each other.

Q: Why is spiritual development difficult for the house-holder?

MM: We tend to give too much importance to the family and thus we get caught up in problems. If we are less attached and offer the fruit of our actions to the Divine, then obstacles can be observed, witnessed.

Q: How do we judge whether or not a marriage is helping spiritual progress?

MM: When there is no harmony in a marriage there is no growth. Harmony is a sure sign of spiritual well-being. Where there is no jealousy or anger, there is harmony. This is not such a high state, but common sense.

Q: Should we try to recognize the Divine in everyone, even in the very worst criminal?

MM: To see the Divine in everything is best, but it is difficult to do.

Q: Can friendship be an obstacle to spiritual practice?

MM: If you turn your love and affection towards the Divine, then everything will be all right.

B&W No. 7
Pondicherry, India 1979

Q: Is my friend helpful to my sadhana? Should I continue the friendship or avoid it?

MM: It is not necessary to leave the friendship. No human being is perfect. In order to live a harmonious life we have to respect the feelings of others. If we are cooperative with others it is not necessary to live alone to achieve the Divine.

Q: Do your devotees have a special relationship to each other?

MM: There is no special karmic relationship, but they can feel that they are a huge family – children with their Mother.

SEX

MM: Do not confuse human and divine love. Give up desire when it goes by itself. The choice to give up desire should be made from joy, not from suffering. What I want is for you to progress from partial joy to complete and perfect joy.

Q: What should my attitude be to sexuality?

MM: The work is done fastest and most purely if you can live without sex and beyond desire. But very few manage that and for many it is extremely dangerous to try to transcend sexuality before they are ready. What is essential is not to renounce it, but to offer it.

Q: I feel ready to give up sex. But I have heard that giving up sex can be dangerous. What do you think?

MM: If the decision to give up sex comes truly from within yourself, it is all right.

Q: Many persons longing for spiritual life have questions about sexuality. Should those who enter on the spiritual way exclude sexuality from their life?

MM: Sexuality is not at all important in spirituality. A spiritual person may choose to have or not to have sexual relations. Spirituality and sexuality are different things.

Q: What do you think about the various relationship choices available – married, single, homosexual and so on?

MM: In general, a man who is a man has a family life. People who believe that sex between men and women is wrong should not think that homosexuality or masturbation is better or spiritually superior – this is incorrect. Sex is sex.

Q: Does sexual bliss help people to understand spiritual bliss?

MM: No. This idea is fundamentally wrong. The pleasure generated between two persons has no spiritual meaning.

Q: Can sex be a path to enlightenment?

MM: Not by itself. What is important is to have sincere devotion to the Divine. Whether you are married or celibate depends on your relationship to the Divine. Marriage is no bar to enlightenment. If marriage is in your karma, you will not escape it.

Q: Can married devotees offer to you their love-making? Will this make it holy?

MM: Yes. Everything can be offered. If they really offer, the blessing is there.

CHILDREN

Q: What is the best way to teach children about God?

MM: It is not necessary to teach children – the awareness of God is in the blood. Often children receive more of the Light because they are more open.

Q: How can we encourage the spirituality of our children?

MM: If they wish, parents can teach the children their own path, whatever it may be.

Q: My daughter is seven years old. Is this too early to teach a child about the Divine?

MM: Don't force her, but you can teach. She is too young to be taught meditation, however. You can do this when she is around twelve years old.

Q: When does the soul enter a fetus?

MM: It depends on the will of the incarnating entity and also the parents' thoughts about the child.

Q: What do you think about abortion?

MM: All the causes of the loss of pregnancy could be considered abortion. We cannot generalize that abortion is good or bad; it depends on circumstance and motivation. Having too many children may mean poverty for a family or a lack of education. This would be a punishment for the other children. In general, it is not good to force people to have unwanted babies.

Q: Is there a significance to being born as a twin?

MM: In one life the two people experienced great pain when they were separated, so now they incarnate together.

Q: When my child was very depressed I prayed to take on his depression. Soon he got better and I fell into a deep depression. Is it possible that I actually took on his depression?

MM: Yes. This sort of thing happens, particularly with parents and their children.

Q: What happens to the karma of a person if someone takes on his pain? How does he then learn the lesson intended by the painful event?

MM: He will still have to go through the pain at some point. The best thing to do is to pray to the Divine for help.

Q: What is the point, then, in taking on the suffering of others if they must still go through the suffering later?

MM: When people live together in a family, it is common that the suffering of one will be taken on by others. If a person has a depressive condition, for instance, it will come again and again. If the parent takes on much of the depression, the child won't have to suffer so much now. When the depressions return, he will have had some relief, so dealing with them will be easier.

THE EMOTIONS

Q: What are the virtues and dangers of the emotions?

MM: Generally, emotions are superficial, on the surface, and they block a deeper entry into oneself. In this sense, there is no advantage, only disadvantage to emotions. They disturb one's ability to be peaceful.

Q: It seems one needs serenity in facing the events that confront us in life.

MM: It is very important. You must be calm. Nothing must frighten you; nothing you experience or feel should shake you. To be like that, you have to turn your whole concentration towards God.

Q: Fear seems terribly destructive. Is there any value to it at all?

MM: When we are afraid we ask for divine help, so fear helps us to remember the Divine.

Q: What is the importance of humor on the path?

MM: It is as much a part of life as sorrow or anything else. Those who have humor may more easily see their own faults.

Q: Westerners are taught to be tough, in the belief that this will make them strong.

MM: But tough is not strong. Love makes you strong. Only the love that is rooted in God is strong – it can bear anything.

Q: People in the West seem so intolerant of each other.

MM: People in India, far more than here in the West, accept each other's weaknesses. In India, if someone is not strong, he does not have to be. If one person is mentally weak, that is accepted. There is a place for everyone.

Q: I feel ashamed of this anger I have for someone.

MM: What use is shame? You must look at this anger simply. It is best not to get angry at all, but if you have to get angry, try to give your anger as a gift. If the person does not change, detach yourself calmly from him or her, and abandon your anger. Whatever you do, do not get absorbed in it.

Q: The Dalai Lama has written that we should especially respect our enemies for they teach us patience and forgiveness. Is this true?

MM: Jesus said this also and it is a great truth. It is easy to love your friends. When you find deep compassion in your heart for your enemies, you are really making progress and learning the power of love.

Q: What should I do with my negative feelings?

MM: You can offer all good and bad to me. It is better not to dwell on the wrong things you have done; you must go on and try to do better next time. Hating bad people will not change them – loving them changes them.

Q: When people hurt me what should I do?

MM: Pray immediately that they should change, and send them love. Your pain will become joy. This is a very powerful method of transforming the ego.

Q: What can one do when one's mind is filled with negative thoughts that keep going endlessly?

MM: Never forget to pray to God. They will end.

No. 25
New York City, USA 1989

FOOD

Q: Do you recommend a vegetarian diet?

MM: I do not ask devotees not to eat meat. If meat suits someone's body, helping it to be strong, then eating it is not wrong. In general, if something suits your body, then you should eat it. To be spiritual it is not necessary to destroy all desire. The fulfillment of those desires that strengthen you and make others happy is good. Which desires should be fulfilled varies from person to person.

Q: But the eating of meat involves hurting of animals.

MM: Some paths say that cutting vegetables hurts them. We must eat in order to survive – it is a circle. If some people don't eat meat they will suffer – so there is suffering in either case.

Q: Is it helpful to do ascetic practices such as fasting?

MM: Fasting is not useful for the spiritual path. But if someone eats too much it is better to reduce the amount consumed, for physical purposes.

Q: How does food affect us?

MM: You must decide what you like to eat; it doesn't affect the attainment of the spiritual goal.

DEATH AND REINCARNATION

Q: How can we prepare for death? Is dying different for those people who have followed a spiritual path?

MM: Don't dwell on death; we can't really prepare. But while living we should do as much japa as possible and remember the Divine – this is helpful to make death go smoothly. The sweetness of the Divine will continue after death. As for those who have not followed a spiritual path, at death it is possible for them to realize how precious God is and how empty their lives have been. If their dying aspiration for God is strong enough, the result can be the same as that of a quester. Perhaps in previous lives these people practiced strongly, and this comes forward in death. Then they have the possibility of realizing the Divine.

Q: How can we help people when they are dying?

MM: Pray that they will have a peaceful existence after death.

Q: At the time of death, where do we go?

MM: Wherever we want to go we will go. The wish at the time of death and the past actions of the lifetime determine future experience.

Q: Will we be conscious of your help in the after-death state?

MM: Yes, I will help in the after-death state and you will be aware that it is I who is helping.

Q: What happens to the soul after death?

MM: The soul continues to develop in the after-death state. After death some souls go straight to the Divine, while most have attachment to the body and consequently are born into a physical body again. Because one cannot fulfill one's desires in the subtle world, as long as one has desires one must take a body again. Some developed souls, such as Mr. Reddy, may keep their perfected subtle bodies so as to help others.

Q: What is the main figure in your paintings of the after-death states?

MM: What is depicted is the form of Mr. Reddy's soul, its subtle body of light. I simply paint what I see.

Q: What is the effect of suicide on one's karma?

MM: Suicide does not stop the work that has to be done in this life – the work will have to continue in the next life. It is better to complete what one needs to do now in this life. In suicide, the body dies but the personality is restless and this restless condition continues into the next birth.

Q: Is it better to bury or to cremate a corpse?

MM: From the point of view of the living, it is better to bury the body of a loved one because the presence of a grave allows for a greater feeling of the presence of the dead person than does a small container of ashes. Then remembrance will still live in the mind and heart. However, some religions believe that cremation burns not only the body but also some of the bad karma.

Q: People visit graves of loved ones for years. Isn't this foolish, since the soul may have already incarnated elsewhere?

MM: No, even then something of the person remains – a physical vibration.

Q: Why is it necessary to reincarnate?

MM: We cannot complete the union with the Divine in one life.

Q: I think that in a past life I was a certain historical person that I read about. Is it true?

MM: No. You have that feeling simply because you have some relation to that person.

Q: What were my past lives like?

MM: Forget the past. Live in the present and remember the Divine.

SIN

Q: What is sin?

MM: There is only one sin, and that is not to love enough.

Q: What is the worst sin?

MM: To hate your neighbors or others, to ill-treat and not respect their feelings.

Q: Assuming that we come from the Divine, where does the urge to sin come from?

MM: We always forget that we are part of the Divine; we give importance to the ego. We believe in self-importance and thus are subject to sin. If you remember the Divine – not only the Divine in yourself, but the complete Divine – you won't sin.

Q: What is the source of sin?

MM: To forget the complete Divine causes sin. The Divine is omnipotent, omniscient.

Q: Does Mother forgive sins?

MM: Everybody should forgive. If we do not forgive, we cannot be called human; forgiveness is a fundamental quality of being a human being. Forgiveness is as important as love. However, laws and punishment are necessary to maintain order in society.

Q: Christ saved thieves and prostitutes. Does the Avatar have the power to change an extraordinary variety of people?

MM: Yes, the Avatar has the power to change anyone and alter any karma.

Q: How can someone who has done wrong open to God?

MM: Aspiration and repentence can change anything.

Q: So it is not what one has done that really matters, but the depth of one's devotion to God?

MM: Even though the thief or prostitute does bad things, he or she may give a pure moment of concentration and devotion to the Divine. This moment is more valuable than hours of sitting in meditation dreaming of other things. It is not the quantity of time devoted to God that is important, but the intensity and quality.

EVIL FORCES

Q: Is there a force that works against the Divine?

MM: Yes.

Q: Do evil powers have control of the world?

MM: The Divine is in control. The Divine knows how to use evil. The evil forces are very dangerous, but very stupid. Never be afraid of evil – even under the worst circumstances. The Divine is always there, always helping – this can be experienced. Evil is real, but not the final reality. The final reality is the Light and love of God. Root yourself in that final reality always and at every moment, and evil will crumble around you.

Q: Why is there evil in the world?

MM: This is due to heartlessness. When the heart grows then there is generosity.

Q: What is the purpose of the existence of evil?

MM: To help man grow. To help man develop. To face man with the consequences of his own choices. To make him turn away from the toys of the world and look for his real self, his real nature.

Q: Can there be any positive result from evil action?

MM: By doing evil, the evil man may wake up. All things are possible.

Q: What do you feel when you see a person who has done many terrible things?

MM: I see not only one person there, but many persons behind – the whole picture must be considered. My love is for all – I love both good and bad people.

Q: If Hitler and Saddam Hussein came to you would you give them darshan?

MM: Yes.

Q: Do you have experience with demons?

MM: Yes, but it is of concern for those who are working with the Light. It is not necessary to explain this to humans. It is a concern for the Divine. To ward off demons, have faith in the Divine. That is all you need.

No. 6
Montreal, Canada 1979

SCIENCE, TECHNOLOGY AND THE FUTURE

Q: What is your attitude to Western technology?

MM: What is important is not to refuse what the West has accomplished – it has accomplished great things in medicine, in physics, in science, in technology – but to direct these from a higher consciousness, to turn all this knowledge to help the world to save itself.

Q: Haven't the use of science and the false belief in its power been very dangerous?

MM: To believe in any power but that of the Divine is dangerous. But all powers can be useful when they are informed with divine awareness, guided by love. Science is a great thing, and some of the greatest scientists are close to the Divine. If they made just one step towards the Light, the Light would reveal itself to them. The greatest scientists are humble – perhaps more humble than artists and philosophers – because they are used to what they cannot see. And because what they are discovering is revealing mystery after mystery to them.

Q: *Will scientists cease their stance as the bearers of wisdom and realize that God exists?*

MM: Many scientists are receiving my Light. Science will not continue as it has; there will be a natural progression toward a more spiritual approach.

Q: *Will man's future evolution thousands of years from now be very different?*

MM: Humans will remain similar but the technology will be different.

Q: *In the future, will the world still be material?*

MM: There will always be matter. But inside us there will be more love.

WORLD CRISIS

Q: *Is this a particularly dangerous moment for the Earth?*

MM: There are always some problems, but there is no danger that the world will be destroyed by them.

Q: *It seems that major desicions on a world scale about the environment and nuclear weapons will have to be made within the next 20 years for humans to have a chance of survival. Is this so? Will these be made?*

MM: The Divine will always give protection. Humans make many mistakes but God protects, helps, pardons and excuses them. That is the way of the Divine.

Q: What about nuclear destruction?

MM: When the divine grace is on man, no man-made creative energy can destroy the world. God is not blind and watches the situation. The destruction of humankind is a human idea, not the divine idea.

Q: Many people say that a collapse of Western civilization as we know it is coming in the next few years.

MM: There is always change, but no big collapse is coming.

Q: Can the West understand your Light before it is too late?

MM: The West IS understanding. Otherwise, how could I stay in it?

Q: Doesn't the Divine also work through destruction in order to clear the way for something new?

MM: It is not like that. The Divine makes us conscious of our mistakes. Sometimes that hurts. But the Divine does not destroy in the way you suggest – the Divine is love. Ninety-nine percent of the destruction is caused by human beings. People must know their responsibility.

Q: How do you see all the various conflicting peoples of the world?

MM: The world for me is my family. The world really IS a family, only the mind does not yet see it. But people are waking up.

Q: Why do certain countries suffer more than others?

MM: Karma. Even in prosperous countries there is suffering but of a different kind.

Q: Why is there so much suffering in the world?

MM: It is normal, it is usual.

Q: How long will wordly conflicts go on?

MM: As long as there is the world, there will be conflicts – but things are improving.

Q: What about the theory of the group effect, that is, that if enough people meditate at one time in one place, this will protect the environment?

MM: One person can protect the whole world.

Q: How does world peace come about?

MM: World peace is achieved by the Divine.

Q: How can harmony come in the world?

MM: We should not think that our own religion or country is better than another. If we love and respect each individual as he is, harmony will come.

Q: Could you tell me about the critical situations in the world?

MM: How do you know there are critical situations?

Q: I read the newspapers.

MM: If you were to spend the amount of time you spend daily reading the newspapers on praying to the Divine for peace in the world, it would be much better.

Q: Doesn't the imperfection of humans endanger the future of mankind and life on earth?

MM: God created normal human beings, not imperfect ones. But he gives mankind permission to do as it will. As humans grow, they do things according to their own thoughts and not according to God's will. God gives us the chance to use our intellects for harmony; if we misuse them for destructive purposes, God gives us the opportunity to change. God will allow us to continue in this way until the situation becomes critical. Then He will stop us – what we try to do will not work. The Divine will intervene, but not in a destructive way. Divine grace is always operating, but in a crisis the degree of divine intervention is much greater.

Q: Aren't people too helpless to really fight against the media, the politicians, and so on?

MM: People can do a great deal if they turn to the Divine and become a channel for it to act purely through them.

Q: Will there be a real evolutionary leap for man coming out of this crisis?

MM: Man must work for that leap. Man must become conscious, must hunger to change, must desire this leap for it to happen. Aspiration and work are everything. My help is always given, my help and my Light.

Q: What can I do to further world peace?

MM: Pray to Him that there should be peace. Bring down Light into your life so that you can do His work of peace in the world. Understand that the pain of the world will only be healed when the world is transformed in God, and work with all your heart and being that this should be accomplished. Do not be distracted by anything from that work.

HELPING THE MOTHER'S WORK

Q: What can I do to help your work?

MM: Realize yourself.

Q: How can people help your work?

MM: They can help by receiving the Light and letting it change them. They should be peaceful and harmonious. To be harmonious means to be whole; to love others and so enjoy your life; to know yourself and your difficulties and to work with them so you become free and able to help others; to respect the dignity of others. Humility brings harmony. A humble person is integrated with reality and is happy, because humility brings happiness.

When you are open, the Divine can pour itself into you. When you are changed, the Divine can work through you.

Q: Isn't climbing to God like climbing a mountain, with many different paths at the bottom that begin to merge when you approach the summit?

MM: Yes. And when you get to the top of the mountain, then you must go down again and help others up, according to their capacities and strength. There is no rest in this work; the highest serves most lovingly; the wisest listens best; the one who has seen gives his whole life to help others to see. This is the divine way.

B&W No. 8   Mr. Reddy, Mother Meera and Adilakshmi. Pondicherry, India 1979

Mother Meera gives Darshan each Friday, Saturday, Sunday, and Monday. It begins at 7 o'clock in the evening. People should be at the Townhall (Mehrzweckhalle) of Thalheim by 6:30. As space is limited, visitors are requested to call and make a reservation 10-12 weeks in advance. Reservations can be made *only by phone* between 10 a.m. and 4 p.m. seven days a week. All letters to Mother should be in Telugu (Mother's native language), English, or German.

Mother Meera's permanent address is:

Oberdorf 4a
65599 Dornburg-Thalheim
Germany
Phone +49-(0)6436-2305
Fax +49-(0)6436-2361
CompuServe: 100342,2574

The following books about Mother Meera are available at the above address:

Answers, by Mother Meera,
in English, German and French
The Mother, by Adilakshmi,
in English, German and French
Bringing Down the Light – Paintings by Mother Meera
Photos of Mother Meera in sizes 10x15 cm, 15x20 cm, and 20x30 cm are also available.

Directions to Mother Meera's Home

Dornburg is a group of 5 villages 15 km north of the town of Limburg, situated between Frankfurt and Cologne (Köln). Visitors must make their own hotel booking. Please come dressed normally, with washed hair, and arrive at the car park at the «Mehrzweckhalle» (town hall, salle polyvalente) in Thalheim by 18.30 (6:30 p.m.). This is the meeting point for all visitors. Do not park anywhere else. Do not go to the houses in the villages and ask for rooms or information. Children are not allowed to come; they get Mother's blessings through their parents. Visitors should be able to sit quietly for three hours. Mother gives answers through the secretary by phone from 16.00 to 17.00 hrs (4 p.m. to 5 p.m.) on Fri, Sat, Sun & Mon.

Travelling by train: Tickets to Limburg, Hadamar, Dornburg-Frickhofen, Wilsenroth and Willmenrod can be purchased at the «Travel center» below airport terminal B. 1) Shuttle train: airport – Frankfurt central station 2) Frankfurt – Limburg: some direct trains or with an easy change across the platform at Niedernhausen 3) Local train: Limburg – your destination.

Bus Nr. 4280 departs opposite Limburg train station (near church) via Hadamar-Niederzeuzheim-Dornburg villages. During the week the bus leaves Limburg about once every hour. On Saturday and Sunday there is less frequent service, please check time table.

Travelling by car: If you want to rent a car it is advisable to negotiate the price at home before you come. It takes 1 hour to drive from Frankfurt airport to Dornburg. Follow signs A3 (Autobahn no.3) to Wiesbaden/ Cologne (Köln), exit Limburg Nord.

From Frankfurt City follow signs A66 Wiesbaden, A3 Cologne (Köln) 80km to Limburg, exit Limburg Nord B54 towards Siegen.

From Limburg: Road B54 to Siegen, exit Dornburg/Hadamar.

From Cologne (Köln): Autobahn A3 towards Frankfurt, 100km to Limburg, Exit Limburg Nord B54 towards Siegen.

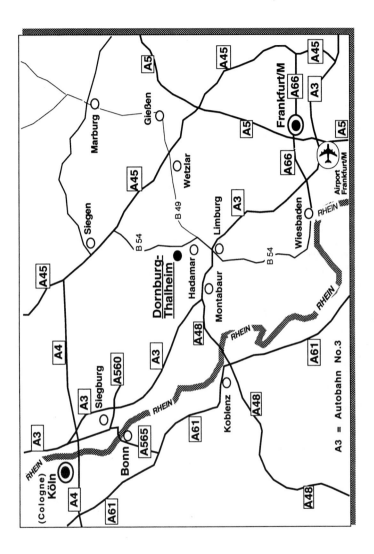

Question: I want to devote my life to you, Mother Meera!

Mother Meera: It is not necessary to devote or believe in me. If you are sincere to your guru, master, God, Absolute or to the Divine, it is enough and I will strengthen your faith. Finally, if you believe in God, that is enough for me. I suggest that you do your job and your duties wholeheartedly and joyfully and bring peace and happiness in your family and in your surroundings; do Japa, the chanting or repeating of the name of God (or whatever you believe in), and ask for whatever you want.

If you need me or my help I will help you, whatever path you may follow. For me there is no difference. All paths lead to the same goal, that is, to realize the Divine.

Question: That means you never encourage us to leave our jobs, families, or countries?

Mother Meera: Yes. That is true. I suggest that people stay where they are. If they need help, I will help them. The help will go without miles counting.